Raves for Dr. Susan Block's *10 Commandments of Pleasure*

"Any man who follows Dr. Block's *10 Commandments of Pleasure* will have women eating out of his hand. Any woman who follows Dr. Block's *10 Commandments of Pleasure* will have men groveling at her feet. . . . Women always ask me what they're doing wrong. Now they can find out by reading Dr. Susan Block. . . . What your mother didn't know about sex and wouldn't have told you if she did. I'll recommend Dr. Block's *10 Commandments of Pleasure* to all my clients who want to know how to be great lovers."
—Dr. Tracy Cabot, author of *How to Make a Man Fall in Love with You*

"Dr. Susan Block's *10 Commandments of Pleasure* is playful, profound, and utterly sensible—a charmingly taught cure for sexual stupidity that is bound to raise the nation's erotic IQ."
—Carol Queen, author of *Exhibitionism for the Shy*

"If you require a new suit, you seek out a great tailor. If you need surgery, you track down the finest doctor. If you want to untangle personal problems, you visit a psychiatrist. So it should not be any different when it comes to love, sex, and relationships—if you've got questions on those, you seek the best answers. And nobody dishes it up better than Dr. Susan Block."
—Robin Leach, television host of *Lifestyles*

"Kudos to Dr. Block for sharing her wisdom with those who wish to develop richer and more fulfilling intimate relationships. It should be required reading for all those people who wish to be regarded as sexually literate. I learned a lot and can honestly say that these commandments are the best to come around in the past two thousand years. Bravo!"
—Nina Hartley, adult film actress

"A must-read for all men aspiring to superpotency, and the women who love them."
—Dr. Dudley Danoff, Beverly Hills urologist and author of *Superpotency*

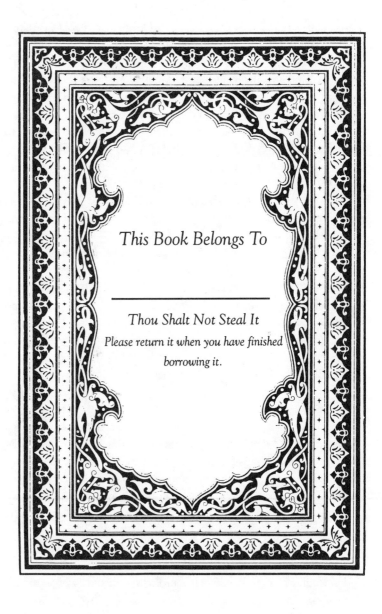

This Book Belongs To

_____

Thou Shalt Not Steal It
Please return it when you have finished
borrowing it.

The

10

COMMANDMENTS

of

PLEASURE

Erotic Keys

to a Healthy Sexual Life

DR. SUSAN BLOCK

ST. MARTIN'S PRESS ❧ NEW YORK

DESIGN BY SONGHEE KIM

Library of Congress Cataloging-in-Publication Data

Block, Susan.
    The 10 commandments of pleasure   /   by Susan Block.
       p.   cm.
    Includes bibliographical references.
    ISBN 0-312-14429-6
    1. Sex.   2. Pleasure.   I. Title.
HQ21.B73   1996   95-48484
306.7—dc20   CIP

First Edition: May 1996
10 9 8 7 6 5 4 3 2 1

Dedicated to the memory of my father,
the inspiration of my mother, the example of my brother,
and the miraculous love of my husband, butler, lover,
muse, coconspirator, and friend, a true prince
among gentlemen, my darling primemate,
Max.

Contents

The

10

COMMANDMENTS

of

PLEASURE

A Prescription for Pleasure

*Hi . . . I'm Dr. Susan Block, your Love Doctor . . . your Mother
Confessor . . . your Baby Girly Girl . . . your Ever-So-Slightly
Twisted Little Sister . . . your Daughter of the American
Revelation . . . your Horny Housewife . . . your Mistress of the
Airwaves . . . your Designated Driver Through the Intoxicating
World of Human Sexuality . . . your Captain of the Ship of Fools
for Love . . . your Leader of the Bonobo Gang . . . and your
Friend—always your Friend. . . .*

As those of you who know me know, that's how I introduce my radio
show. Every week for over ten years, I've broadcast live on the air to
millions of you via microphones all over the world—from a tiny stu-
dio in Redondo Beach to a chic salon in Paris, from an underground
club in San Francisco to a hotel (on Max's and my wedding night!)
in Philadelphia, from a language school in Stuttgart to my trademark
"boudoir bully pulpit," my very own big brass bed.

I broadcast the show from bed because what better place to talk
about sex? I know that those of you who listen, or watch me on the
TV version of the show, from *your* beds can appreciate the intimacy,
eroticism, and sheer fun of that. You who have listened, watched, at-

tended my seminars, sat on my famous couch for therapy, called me, chatted with me in cyberspace, and sent thousands of letters (not to mention a few charmingly explicit photos) are the inspiration for this book of pleasures.

You have joined me in my celebrations and supported me in my struggles. You have played with me, prayed with me, and stayed with me. When I've been kicked off one station for speaking "too" openly about sex, you have searched your radio dial and found me on another (maybe officially, or perhaps being "pirated" by mischievous board operators). You have shared with me your deepest secrets and passions, your amazing fantasies and extraordinary realities. I dedicate to you, my darling reader—and you know who you are—these *10 Commandments of Pleasure* . . . which are really twenty commandments, connecting the two better halves of humanity: The 10 Commandments of a Lady's Pleasure and The 10 Commandments of a Gentleman's Pleasure. Together, these twenty laws of love and pleasure embody a code that I call *ethical hedonism,* an erotic etiquette to guide you (and me) toward fully and dramatically expressing our sexual, animal nature, while maintaining the peace as civilized, considerate ladies and gentlemen.

These are twenty Pleasure Principles to give and receive by, composed with care, passion, laughter, a little sweat, a few tears, a lot of orgasms, and the divine inspiration of the spirits. They are for all of us—couples and singles, conservative and liberal, radical and traditional, the young and the old, the hip and the geeky, dealmakers and homemakers, professors and truckers, ministers and rabbis, priests and high priestesses, coppers, rockers, rappers, and grandmothers.

They will give you pleasure. They will give you power. Most important, they will give you the power to *give* pleasure.

The Power to Give Pleasure Is the Greatest Power You Have.

My husband Max and I have lived and loved by these commandments for almost a decade. They are simple, universal, playful, and, like the original Ten, they are powerful. Best of all, they work. Study them, live by them, love by them, and you have a very good chance of finding, and actually staying in, a romantic paradise—your Land of Milk and Honey.[1]

With pleasure,
Susan Marilyn Block, Ph.D.

[1]"The Land of Milk and Honey" is another phrase for "The Promised Land" (see Deuteronomy 6:3 in your Bible). It is first and foremost a spiritual paradise, but it is also, according to my own exotic erotic interpretation, a sexual one where milk (male semen) and honey (female juices) are mingled in harmony and abundance.

How to Use This Book

This book is interactive. It plays with you. It is a pleasure workbook. You can begin at the beginning and read it straight through as you would a "normal" book. You can start at the end (some people like to learn backwards). Or you can go instantly to the commandment that intrigues you most, and just pick up the others when you feel the need or curiosity.

For the Serious Reader
If you're interested in what these commandments are based upon—the origins of love, the politics of pleasure, and my philosophy of *ethical hedonism*—read through this Prescription for Pleasure first. Then go through the commandments in their proper order.

Advice for the Attention Span–Impaired
If you have the attention span of a gnat (or a Hollywood executive), and don't usually read anything but *TV Guide* or the trades, no problem! Just skip my prescription for now (you'll sneak peeks at it later), and check the table of contents for the commandments that really touch your heart or tickle your genitalia. For instance, if you're interested in giving a lady pleasure through oral sex (and who isn't?), go straight to Lady's Commandment #9: Thou Shalt Have Foreplay (page 59).

After each set of commandments, you'll find an abbreviated version of all ten for quick and easy referral. I call them Lo-Cal Commandments—no fat, no cholesterol, no footnotes, and suitable for framing, hanging on bedroom or bathroom walls, or keeping under pillows.

Also, you'll notice that I sometimes cross-refer from one commandment to another. If you follow the references, you'll probably wind up reading all the commandments pretty thoroughly even though you didn't do it from beginning to end and didn't think you had much of an attention span. See, you're already improving!

Now let's take a little pleasure trip. . . .

The Bonobo Way

Deep in the soul of the hot, wet swamps of Zaire, there is a tribe. It is here, in their wild, erotic Garden of Eden, that our closest cousins, the bonobos (pronounced *bon-'oh-bows*), live and share a powerful kind of pleasure, and make an extraordinary kind of love.

The Horniest Chimps on Earth

Bonobos, also called pygmy chimpanzees (*Pan paniscus*), are as close to human as primates can get. They have longer legs than common chimps, more open faces with higher foreheads and other characteristics that place them closer in appearance to humans. The genitals of bonobo females are rotated forward like those of human females, so that they can have face-to-face sex rather than just "doggy-style," with the male mounting from behind like most other primates. Basically, bonobos can do "it" in almost as many positions as we can, and they *do* do it—a lot.

Bonobos have some kind of sex almost every day. Females are in heat for three-quarters of their cycle, and many of them copulate even when not in heat, a sexual pattern more like human females than that of any other mammal. Though common chimpanzees only have sex to reproduce, bonobos share all kinds of sexual pleasures, including cunnilingus, fellatio, masturbation, massage, bisexuality, body licking, sex in different positions, group sex, and lots of long, deep, wet, soulful French kissing. Like tantric sex practitioners, or just like two people very much in love, copulating bonobos often look deeply into each other's eyes. Such loving passion, such sexual dexterity, such clever, horny playfulness is found nowhere else on earth except among humans.

Using Pleasure to Create Peace

But that's not all that make our kissin' cousins, the bonobos, so worthy of our attention. It's not just how they *have* sex, but how they *use* sex—to ease stress, to maintain relationships, as a form of commercial exchange (e. g., I'll give you a kiss if you give me a banana), and *to reduce violent conflict.*

Scientific observation has revealed that social interactions among bonobos are far less hostile than among common chimps. This is not to say that bonobos never fight—they just do so a lot less—and unlike common chimps (and humans), bonobos have never been observed deliberately killing members of their own species. Also unlike common chimps, their social organization is not male-dominated; females play important social roles. Among bonobos observed both in the wild and in captivity, sex and mutual pleasure are vital keys to keeping the peace, reinforcing social relations based upon the give and take of sensual, erotic pleasure rather than on pain and force and fear.

Apparently, all that good sex just cools them out.

"The Bonobo Way" is a very simple philosophy (after all, these aren't geniuses, darling, they're chimpanzees!) that we all *know* deep in our bones, but that we seem to forget in the midst of our busy, lonely, fearful, stressful, polluted, violent lives:

> *Pleasure Eases Pain* * *Good Sex Defuses Tension* *
> *Love Lessens Violence* * *And You Can't Very Well Fight a War*
> *While You're Having an Orgasm.*

The "commandments" in this book are my way of applying the principles of the Bonobo Way to the far more complex, civilized lives of human ladies and gentlemen. They support the repression of violence and the free, exuberant, erotic, raunchy, loving, peaceful, consensual expression of pleasure. They will teach you not only to find the pleasures in your life, but to share them with your "primemate,"[1] your beautiful bonobo partner-in-love.

---

[1] I created the term *primemate,* based on a combination of the words *prime* and *mate,* and a play on the word *primate.* I use it throughout this book to mean "lover" or "partner," "husband" or "wife." Basically, your primemate is your prime mate (usually your only mate, though not necessarily).

Why Commandments of Pleasure?

The wild and free Bonobo Way only goes so far for us big-brained folk. Freedom is vital to love and pleasure, but the human animal needs laws to live by, and also to love by. We need structure, guidance, rules, commandments. And we have all of that. Probably, we have far too much of all of that. Yet something essential is missing. The multitude of state and religious laws and commandments pertaining to sexuality are all about *restricting* sexuality. The commandments in this book are all about *enhancing* sexuality. Other laws and commandments invoke and perpetuate guilt and shame. These commandments invoke and inspire love and pleasure.

According to the Bible, God gave Moses the original Ten Commandments because the Children of Israel had been slaves in Egypt for more than four hundred years, and then suddenly they were free. The newly freed slaves needed the guidance of the commandments because they were wandering in a wilderness. The physical wilderness of their harsh desert environment challenged their ability to survive, while the social wilderness of these virtually lawless tribes challenged their ability to get along.

Over the last few decades of the twentieth century, tremendous cultural and technological changes have freed modern women and men from old shackles of sexual repression, then challenged us to survive and get along. Before the sexual and feminist revolutions, most men and (especially) women were slaves to their marriages—good or evil—just as the Children of Israel were slaves to the pharaohs of Egypt. Freedom threw modern women and men out into "the wilderness," a feral terrain of extramarital sex, divorce, abandonment, variety, violence, competition, discourtesy, almost infinite possibility, and profound confusion: a brave new battleground of the sexes, and a brand-new challenge for society.

For years now, women and men have been wandering through this wilderness of broken rules, broken homes, broken dreams, and far too many broken noses. We are "crying out"—like the Children of Israel—for well-lit signs to guide us along the path of our pleasures without raising roadblocks to our freedoms. We don't want to return to being slaves to bad marriages and bankrupt moralities. Despite intense pressures from the Old Religious Right and the New Religious

Left to return to the spurious "safety" of sexual slavery, most of us will not give up our freedom to live and love as we choose.

But freedom without law is mayhem. Everyone knows that, everyone feels it. People want and need "laws" of pleasure that can balance respect and culture with desire and fulfillment. In that spirit, I present these two sets of 10 Commandments of Pleasure. Laws that neither Moses, the Pope, the Ayatollah, the President, nor the Speaker of the House would ever give you. Laws that no police officer need enforce. Laws that are truly a pleasure to follow, and not such a sin to transgress. Laws that—if you really follow them—will lead you to the Promised Land:

> *We are the Lord and Lady,*
> *Thy God and Goddess, King and Queen of the Universe,*
> *who, with strong hands and outstretched arms,*
> *brought you out of the land of repression*
> *into this earthly paradise of pleasure.[2]*
> *Amen. . . . And A-women, too!*

What Is Pleasure?

Pleasure[3] is being pleased. Plump with satisfaction. Full of joy. Ecstatic. Orgasmic. Excited, aroused, yet at the same time secure, taken care of. In Greek mythology, *Pleasure* is the name of the beautiful, beloved daughter of *Eros* (Erotic Love) and *Psyche* (Soul). Pleasure is gratification—instant, delayed, or diffused. Pleasure is being in love. Pleasure is savoring lust. Pleasure is the smell of your primemate's hair, the look in her eyes, the touch of his tongue, the taste of her skin, the sound of his voice whispering in your ear. Pleasure is petting. Pleasure is being stroked. Pleasure is laughing so hard your face hurts. Pleasure is being teased with love. Pleasure is physical, emotional, intellectual, spiritual. Pleasure is sexual. Pleasure can be peaceful, and it can be dangerous. There is pleasure in power, and pleasure in surrender. There is sometimes pleasure in pain. There is pleasure in being held tight, in the warm strong arms of your gentleman or the hot wet womb of your lady. And there is pleasure in doing the holding.

---

[2]This is my couple-oriented, nonpatriarchal, pleasure-positive adaptation of the First Commandment (which is actually more of a declaration than a law) of the biblical Ten. Check your Bible (Exodus 20:1–17) for the original Ten.

[3]For etymology fetishists, the root of *pleasure* is the French *plaisir*.

Our pleasures are as different as our DNA and as similar as our common ancestors, whom anthropologists believe lived and loved somewhere in Africa hundreds of thousands of years ago.

The Value of Pleasure

Everyone (except maybe die-hard ascetics) agrees that pleasure is nice and all, but isn't it far too frivolous a matter to require such serious injunctions as commandments? After all, pleasure is hardly ever front-page news as pain and violence are. Pain is studied, broadcast, analyzed, dramatized, glorified, worried over. Pain is big business. Pleasure is something to *maybe* get into on the weekend, after a full week of pain, during your time off (*what* time off?).

To me, pleasure is very serious. And it should be to you, too. Why? Pleasure is what keeps us going, literally and figuratively. It's not just good for us; it's good for everyone around us. The cultivation of peaceful pleasures quells the impulse to violence (something that could, no doubt, use quite a bit of quelling), and our bonobo cousins aren't the only ones to demonstrate that.

"Activate Your Pleasure Centers"

According to my favorite developmental neuropsychologist, Dr. James Prescott, who studied violence and sexual behavior in forty-nine cultures, "Our brains have a built-in reciprocal relationship between pleasure and violence. When the pleasure systems of the brain are activated, they inhibit the neural systems that mediate violence. So one way to inhibit violence is to activate your pleasure centers."[4]

Yet our society denigrates pleasure, especially *sexual* pleasure. Of course, commercial TV and other media *use* sex—just as they use violence (as well as a horribly distorted mix of sex and violence)—to attract an audience. But very few programs educate audiences about positive, creative approaches to cultivating sexual pleasure. Most of them sensationalize sex and then get all sanctimonious about it, as if to say, "Look at my beautiful sexy body. Oooh, come on, baby, don't you want to look? Of course, you do. . . . Hey, what are *you* looking at? You pervert!" or, "Come here, darling, make love to me. . . . *Now*

[4]From Lyn Ehrnstein, "A Brain-Mind Theory of Culture, Sexuality and Moral Behavior: An Interview with Dr. James Prescott," *Floodtide*. Vol. 3, no. 4 (Summer 1992), p. 2.

you're going to die!" This vividly enticing yet harshly disapproving attitude toward sex reinforces our worst, most shameful feelings about giving and receiving sexual pleasure.

And so, to a great extent, we are becoming a society of chronic sexual screw-ups. Which is very sad. Because we have so much potential to be sexy, peaceful, gracious bonobo ladies and gentlemen.

With very strong values. I'm not talking about "family values," at least not the narrow, paternalistic, 1950s-style family values that politicians swoon over. I'm talking about personal values. The value of pleasure, and not violence. The value of love, and not war. The value of lust, and not greed. The value of knowledge, and not ignorance. The value of sexual connection, and not gender competition. The value of giving, and not holding back.

That's one reason these commandments focus on *sexual* pleasure. Strip away the fear and moralizing, and sexuality is all about creativity, the opposite of destruction. It's a natural tranquilizer, a positive energizer, and a great *equalizer*. Everyone alive can find sexual fulfillment of some sort. So much of our societal ethic is based not on finding pleasure but on "being the best." But not everyone can be the best. Not everyone can be President. Not everyone can be rich. It's just not logistically possible. But everyone who can breathe can experience an orgasm. And everyone can fall in love.

Sexual pleasure with love—the kind of love that cools you out and warms you up—is a healing force. Ultimately, it heals the pain. . . .

But the fact is that it doesn't "just happen" to most of us, at least not for long. It comes and goes like the weather, and most of us feel we have about as much control over our love lives as we do over the weather. But we can use windmills to direct the wind, and we can use these commandments to guide ourselves and our primemates toward the pleasures in life and away from the pain.

Use These Commandments Like a Machete

In my private sex therapy practice, seminars, radio and TV shows,[5] I see and hear so many people who can't connect, so many couples pulling away from each other sexually and emotionally. At first, the pleasure between the couple excites them. Their natural erotic in-

---

[5] I do a lot of stuff.

fatuation is so powerful, it's palpable. Then something happens, they have kids, work gets hard, life gets tough, reality sinks in. And they let the love die. Sex slips away into the corners of their lives. Pleasure—even simple, inexpensive pleasure—becomes a luxury, not a priority. Sometimes, it seems to be an impossibility. Because as soon as the pleasure starts seeping out, it is replaced by some sort of pain. Angry words. Sexual rejection. Blaming looks. Then the pain is what excites and connects the couple. And to find their way back to pleasure, they have to fight through a thicket of pain.

Is the pain obscuring the pleasure in your life?

Use these commandments like a machete—not to hurt anyone, darling, *please*, but to cut through the thicket of personal pain and massive societal misinformation. They will show you a path to a new Land of Milk and Honey flowing and growing right in your own backyard, where you and your primemate(s) can frolic forever.

Pleasure Power

If you read "between the lines" of pleasure, you'll find that this is a book about power.

Essentially, people give you power for two reasons: (1) because they fear you; or (2) because they love you. These commandments will help you to gain power for the second reason. They will teach you to awaken and fulfill erotic desire in others. They will show you how to use your sexual power to give pleasure. Understanding your sexual power and how to use it to give pleasure opens you up to all kinds of possibilities in life—in the bedroom, in the boardroom, on the beach, everywhere.

The giving of pleasure puts you into a powerful position.

The Land of Milk and Honey is flowing before you. If you are an *ethical* hedonist, as I encourage you to be, you will use the power of these commandments with benevolence, peacefulness, and grace.

This Is Not a Self-Help Book

This is not a self-help book in the strict sense of the term, because this is not a book about how to help yourself. It is a book about how to help someone else. Eventually, that helps you, of course. What goes around does come around. Tit for tat, and all of that. But don't give pleasures parsimoniously, with the expectation of immediate reimbursement. Otherwise, you'll never experience the pure, unadulterated rapture of *giving* pleasure.

Sex and God

I don't mean to offend or even amend the original Ten Commandments. For the most part, they still stand up quite well, especially number six.[6] I *do* mean to *extend* them into the realm of pleasure-giving. Even so, you may wonder, how can I mix such a frank, unorthodox discussion of sex with the Ten Commandments, the foundation of Western religion, the purported word of God?

Actually, sex and God have a lot in common. The mystical experience and the erotic experience are the most intense in human life: both connect desire with awe, anguish, fear, pleasure, pain, and extreme logic-defying *passion*. Religious mystics love God with a passion that can be feverishly romantic, and who do most lovers call out to in the throes of erotic passion? God, baby, God, baby, God! And yet, according to certain so-called religious people, sex and God are pretty much at odds.

Why Did God Create the Clitoris?
I believe that the divine God/Goddess/Nature force that created human sexuality made it pleasurable for a reason, not just to "be fruitful and multiply,"[7] but to heal pain, and to physically express spiritual unity. Why else did God create the clitoris, a part of the female body that has no function whatsoever except to experience pleasure? To say in the name of God that "sex is dirty" perpetuates centuries of religiously inspired sexual abuse in homes, churches, and temples, creating intense shame about our desires, fueling the belief that parts of our bodies are dirty, fostering hatred and confusion about pleasure. Of course, the irony of creating a taboo is that, once something is forbidden, it often becomes very interesting. The idea

[6]Thou Shalt Not Kill.
[7]From the story of Noah, Genesis 9:1 in your Bible.

that we're doing something naughty, behind the back of the Lord, so to speak, makes it exciting—*hot*. Our erotic necessity, like Mother Nature, always finds a way to assert itself.

There Is Nothing Unsacred About Sex

And yet there has always been something about sex that subverts institutionalized religion. In medieval times, the songs of the European troubadours virtually deified erotic love between human ladies and gentlemen. This powerful, passionate love was soon seen by the Roman Catholic Church as competition for the affections of the people. If erotic love was not a sin, but the key to the meaning of life, if gentlemen worshipped ladies through song, who would worship God at church? The conflict between love and church[8] was so serious that Crusades were fought over it. The Albigensian Crusade of 1208,[9] one of Europe's most violent Crusades, was launched by Pope Innocent III against the troubadour culture of southern France. Despite the Church's brutal condemnation of love's pleasures, the legacy of the medieval troubadours and trobaritzes[10] has lived on, and their spiritual, courteous, passionate approach to sexuality permeates these Commandments of Pleasure.

Male and Female Pleasures

These commandments are a prescription for peace among weary warriors on the battleground of the sexes. Following them transforms the battleground into a playground. I developed them as "playground rules" for Max and me, as well as in response to various clients, callers, and friends who often ask for guidelines in the giving of pleasure, especially to someone of the "opposite" sex.

The sexes are, in fact, not really opposite. Men are not from Mars, and women are not from Venus. We are both from this beautiful, wild, sexual planet Earth. And we are far more alike—body, mind, and soul—than we are different. As Aristotle pointed out in his *Po-*

---

[8]The French word for love, *amor*, spelled backwards is *roma*, the Roman Catholic Church.

[9]The only Crusade by Christians against Christians.

[10]Medieval ladies who also composed troubadour-style love songs.

etics, long before the advent of feminism, women and men are "on the whole the same."[11]

So why have two sets of Ten Commandments, one for ladies and one for gentlemen? Because it's the damn differences that cause the confusion![12] Based on these few but profound genital, biological, social, and hormonal differences, we must learn how to "do unto others" *not* as we would have others do unto us, but as those others *really* want us to do to them. While women and men are no different in our basic need for sex, love, passion, and pleasure, we have differences in the way that we express and experience these needs. Hence these two sets of commandments, one to help each sex understand what the other really wants and needs when it comes to receiving pleasure.

The Sexes Need Each Other

That's something we are always relearning, isn't it? Men and women don't live very well without each other, so we'd better learn to get along. And learning to give each other pleasure goes a long way toward getting along. For heterosexual couples, these commandments are essential, though flexible, rules to love by. But even gay men and women need to learn to deal with the opposite sex (although they can, if they wish, just follow the commandments for their own sex). The sexes need each other, but we can often use a little help in learning to please each other. These commandments provide a little help, a little encouragement, and a lot of good, clean, sexy (even kinky!) fun.

We All Have Our Masculine and Feminine Sides

The wisdom of many cultures tells us we are all at least somewhat androgynous. The Taoist yin-yang symbol is a black and white circle—black symbolizing the female, and white representing the male. Within the white half of the circle is a black dot, and inside the black half is a white dot, meaning that every male has some female in him and vice versa. C. G. Jung, the founder of analytical psychol-

---

[11]*The Works of Aristotle in Four Parts*, 1822 edition.

[12]Speaking of confusion, one practical reason that I separate these commandments into "Ladies" and "Gentlemen" is that it helps me to keep my pronouns straight without having to say "he or she" or "his or her" a lot.

ogy, called a gentleman's feminine side his "anima" and a lady's masculine side her "animus."[13]

Most of us are bisexual, if not in terms of sexual preference, at least
in terms of our personalities. In many ways, masculinity and femininity are not inevitable roles to which we are eternally bound, but
erotic opportunities for us to experience life and express ourselves.

Also, our ideas of masculine and feminine behavior or style
change as our culture changes. For instance, in eighteenth-century
Western Europe, noblemen wore frilly lace, stockings, high heels,
and beauty marks. Many of our so-called sex differences are actually
quite arbitrary, but we are so conditioned to believe in them as "natural" that they do become part of our natures.

And yet, as you explore the *differences* between women and men
that these commandments are based on, I think you will find the *sim-
ilarities* always lurking between the lines. For instance, both sexes
love to be erotically aroused, which we find under Lady's Commandment #2: Thou Shalt Stimulate Her Senses (page 11) and Gentleman's Commandment #5: Thou Shalt Excite Him (page 123). Both
sexes need positive feedback, which we find under Lady's Commandment #3: Thou Shalt Compliment Her Meaningfully and
Often (page 27) and Gentleman's Commandment #9: Thou Shalt
Regard Him as a Hero (page 163).

> *Which commandments do you most identify with?*
> *What kinds of pleasure do you most desire?*

Some men might identify more with the female commandments
and some women may identify more with the male. If that's true for
you, feel free to cut and paste accordingly. These commandments are
not meant to be absolute, especially not in the shady realm of sex differences.

The Joy of Generalizing
Of course, if we in the field of "pop philosophy" (not to be confused
with pop psychology)[14] didn't allow ourselves to generalize a little

[13]C. G. Jung, "Marriage as a Psychological Relationship," *The Portable Jung*
(New York: Viking Press, 1971), pp. 173–175.
[14]Like the late great Jim Morrison who coined the term, I am an "erotic philosopher."

(or a lot), we'd have nothing to write![15] Thus, these commandments are based upon the general tendencies of women and men, not upon the inevitable exceptions to the rules.

However, having lived most of my own life as an "exception" to a lot of rules, I feel compelled to address those "exceptional" readers: You may very well be a gentleman who needs more foreplay than your female partner; she could be a female ejaculator who gets pleasure out of having you swallow.

There is a God and Goddess in every lady and gentleman. Your best bet is to follow both sets of commandments in order to serve both the feminine and masculine sides of your male or female primemate(s).

Why Commandments for "Ladies" and "Gentlemen"?

Why not the simpler, more basic "women" and "men"? The terms "lady" and "gentleman" came into fashion around the same time that romantic love came into fashion, during that period of the troubadours in the Middle Ages. These times were brutal, in some ways more violent than modern times, though body counts are much higher now since so many people use guns instead of swords.

The troubadours and trobaritzes were the "protesters" of that era. They sang of an ideal male, a "gentle man" who was brave without being a brute, who respected, adored, and practically worshipped the noble lady of his heart's desire. And they sang of a "lady" who was not only beautiful, but spiritual, erotic, and powerful. The lady had much more power in her courtly love relationship with her gentleman than other women who, in those harshly anti-female times, were typically treated as chattel by their families, beaten by their husbands, and raped by knights passing through town. So the lady and gentleman were quite extraordinary human beings of love, passion, and courtesy, beacons of light in dark ages.

Serve Each Other's Pleasures

If our most primal sexual selves are bonobo chimps, happily humping away, perhaps our most civilized sexual selves are ladies and gentlemen serving each other's pleasures with exquisite, erotic manners.

---

[15]It's not only pop philosophers who generalize and issue commandments. "Actual philosophers," wrote Friedrich Nietzsche in *Beyond Good and Evil* (1886), "are commanders and lawgivers: they say 'thus it shall be!'"

Serve Each Other Milk and Honey, Nourishment and Excitement,
with Passion and Courtesy.

The Value of a Good (Sex) Education

As those of you who know me know, I'm a sex educator with a "mission": to wipe out sexual stupidity. Sexual stupidity is at the root of a lot of human problems. And I'm not just talking about not practicing safe sex, though that can be a problem. Sexual stupidity is larger and more pervasive than that. Out of sexual stupidity come prejudice and bigotry, heartache and misery, loneliness and violence.

So, practice your ABCs, darling, learn about computers, study your history, get your M.B.A., J.D., or Ph.D.—they're all important. But get smart about sex.

Of course, the smartest people in any class are the ones who ask the questions, so don't be afraid to ask questions, whether you need to ask your gynecologist, urologist, endocrinologist, cardiologist, or sex therapist a technical question, or to ask your primemate a personal one.

How else are we to learn about sex? Most of our parents don't teach us about sex, except in the vaguest or most moralistic manner. Those school sex ed courses are only on conception and contraception, never on how to keep love alive or give great head. The education we *may* have gotten in the proverbial back alleys of our youth wasn't much better; it just made sex seem dirty and confusing. Fortunately, there are a few places to learn about sex, if you know where to look, such as this book, other sex books, sex educational videos, plus the occasional decent sex educational TV or radio show (like mine). There are even institutes (like mine) where you can study sexology. Of course, the most pleasant place to learn about sex is through your sexiest headmaster or headmistress: your partner-in-love.

And yes, there *is* stuff to learn. After all, sex may be natural—if you're happy being a male premature ejaculator or an inorgasmic woman or a couple that stops having sex after infatuation wears off—but if you want sex to be good, you have to learn a thing or two. As the Latin poet Ovid noted, "Skill makes love unending."[16]

---

[16]Ovid, *Ars Amatoria*, Book 3.

Repression Relies on Ignorance

We need education in the sexual sciences to wipe out damaging, sometimes deadly superstitions and misinformation. We need education in the sexual arts to help improve our erotic lives and to keep our families intact. We need education in sexual psychology and philosophy to help us determine our true sexual nature and to cultivate it in a fulfilling, ethical manner.

Your New Sex Education Begins with "Chemistry" Class . . .

Over the course of evolution, nature has provided us with powerful chemical "rewards" that give us feelings of pleasure when we give and receive love. So, that intense ecstasy we feel when we "fall in love" is not just in our heads, it's in our *genes* (pun intended)! *But* it's not eternal, nor is it exclusive. Long-term monogamous romance is not natural. So, if we want to make it last, it's up to us to *trick nature*.

As we fall in love, we're flooded with amphetaminelike chemicals—including *phenylethylamine* (PEA)—that start in the brain and race along the nerves. These pleasure chemicals are literal painkillers. That's why an orgasm can cure cramps, a hug can ease tension, and a kiss can shoo the blues away much better than a drug. See, love *is* a natural "high." But PEA highs don't last forever. The body builds up a tolerance to PEA, so that euphoric "falling-in-love" feeling dissipates, often spelling the end of romance.

But don't panic! All isn't lost, chemically speaking. Other chemicals, *endorphins,* enter to provide that comfy, old-shoe, in-love feeling. Unlike the fizzy hot PEA, endorphins give longtime lovers a soothing sense of security. Another chemical, *oxytocin,* also flows in during this phase, sensitizing nerves, stimulating muscle contraction, enhancing orgasm, and making cuddling feel delicious. Nature "knows" that, whether we're "in love" or not, a complex species such as ours needs caring touch to survive.

Now you know why you love to cuddle so much!

Yet, with the romantic PEA high gone, many people feel they've "fallen" out of love. From nature's viewpoint, romance merely serves an evolutionary purpose: to exert a powerful enough pull on people so they will do what it takes to procreate. But nature only provided for the feeling to last at most a few years, enough time to rear a child through infancy (at which point, conceivably, the "tribe" would take over raising the now less helpless child). Then, according to nature's probable plan, each adult would find a new partner and start again. That's why we have the "seven-year itch," or as some scientists see it, the "four-year itch,"[17] with divorce rates in most cultures peaking at the fourth year of marriage.

How to Trick Nature

Yet, despite nature, many couples do stay together and even keep the romance blazing between them. How do they do that? The "secret" to keeping the pleasures of love alive long term is this: Cultivate the natural endorphins and oxytocin by doing all you can to make each other feel nice, comfortable, cuddled, and cared for—AND *trick* those amphetaminelike PEA chemicals into kicking in every so often through challenging, surprising, teasing each other, being creative together, and sharing fantasies. How to manage that? Follow the commandments in this book, and you'll keep those endorphins and oxytocins simmering nicely, as well as trick that PEA into erupting enough to make you feel like you're on your first hot date, even if you've been together through twenty years, three kids, two mortgages, and a bankruptcy!

[17]See Helen Fisher, *Anatomy of Love: The Natural History of Monogamy, Adultery and Divorce* (New York: W. W. Norton, 1992), p. 109.

Pre-Commandment Notes to Readers

A Note to Skeptics

Do you scoff at such assertions, darling reader? It's easy to be skeptical about the power of pleasure, to say love doesn't last, that it can't last beyond the seven-year itch, or the six-month scratch, or the two-week tickle. It's not easy to speak up for love—true, romantic love that's both hot and warm—without sounding like some sort of deluded, born-yesterday *fool* for love.

But even skeptics fall in love. And some even stay in love—either with well-matched partners-in-skepticism or with unwavering optimists who have a great sense of humor. But some don't or can't, and Lord knows, they're right: There *are* plenty of phonies out there, plenty of bad breaks for good people, lots of obstacles on the road of a long and pleasurable life together. But don't let that discourage you. Consider the wise words of that horny old Victorian, William Thackeray:

> *To love and win is the best thing;*
> *To love and lose, the next best thing.*

And consider this, my darling skeptic: It's never too late to share the pleasure in your life.

A Note to True Lovers

The good news is: True love exists. And it doesn't stink. In fact, it's the greatest. And you can have it in your life—hot, sexy, lip-locking, butt-spanking, nipple-squeezing, love-button-pushing, pleasure-sharing, pain-healing, passionate, compassionate, twenty-four-hours-a-day, seven-days-a-week, fifty-two-weeks-a-year, every year, for years and years, TRUE love—despite what the skeptics say.

But if you have true love in your life, you can't have anything else. That's why so many of us can't hold on to it. True love is like a god or goddess, a thing within us to be worshipped, and like most gods, it is a jealous god. It demands your devotion. You can't go halfway with true love. If you try, it will abandon you, slap you in the face, ruin your life, or just leave you bored and lonely and wondering: Where has love gone? What happened to the romance? If you want to find and keep true love in your life, it must be your top priority. No ifs, ands, buts, or doubts. Make love *first* if you want to make love *last*. That's all there is to it, but that's a lot. That's too much for most people.

Does all this sound like love addiction? Like *codependency?* "Codependency," a perfectly lovely concept, has become not only a dirty word in the limited lexicon of "support-speak," it's virtually a crime, a sin, a weakness, a failing, a *problem*. Entrepreneurial psychobabblists with troubled pasts promise cures for codependency, like snake-oil salesmen promising to cure what ails you, like bomb-happy generals promising to win the war even though they destroy the country. The War on Codependency and lovers who "love too much" is a war against passion, pleasure, and love. As the English writer and onetime doctor W. Somerset Maugham said:

> *"The great tragedy of life is not that men perish,*
> *but that they cease to love."*

The War on Codependency is big business, because who can't relate to the symptoms? Who has not suffered at some point from the deep sweet agony and ecstasy of love addiction? Of course, any addiction—to love or anything else—can have negative consequences, ranging from separation anxiety to murder, if a toxic combination of character and circumstances comes into play. But codependency in itself is not a bad thing. It's not "dysfunctional." There's nothing wrong with being addicted to love.

Just don't get addicted to loving a jerk.

Loving, needing, and depending on others and having them love, need, and depend on you is a good thing, a healing thing. It's the best thing. Going out of your way to give pleasure to someone you care about is not bad for you. It will not turn you into a wimp. It will strengthen you and your relationship.

Love in Action

Love is not just something we feel, it's something we do. What difference does it make if someone "loves" you if they treat you badly? *True love is in action.* The commandments in this book help you pleasure each other in and out of bed, and cultivate a *healthful* obsession for each other. Notice that all commandments are in the positive. There are no "Thou Shalt Nots." All provide positive *actions* for you to express your love.

One way to actively love someone is to help them succeed in loving you. Check off the commandments that are really important to you before giving this book to your primemate. Help him or her to love and pleasure you. If he or she isn't ready to read this book for some reason, just leave it around the bedroom or bathroom; your curious primemate won't be able to resist a look.

Love is not a prerequisite for following the commandments in this book. You don't have to be in love to give and receive pleasure. But love does help to make it all more worthwhile.

Love is the dressing in the salad of pleasures.

If you haven't yet found it, these commandments will help you find your way to true love. If you have, they will help you hold on to it. "Love is all we have," wrote Euripides of ancient Greece, "the only way that each can help the other."

"Love is supreme and unconditional," said jazz great Duke Ellington, "*like* is nice but limited." Don't limit yourself, darling . . . Open yourself up to love—it's the only way it can enter your life. It *can* enter your life.

A Note to Monogamous Couples

In nature, monogamy is rare. The Nile crocodile, the American toad, the wood roach, the reedbuck, muskrats, most birds, some bats, beavers, a few monkeys, some wild dogs, and the ironically named dik-dik are monogamous creatures—at least, they're into serial monogamy. Monogamy is not the norm in nature, since it's not normally to a male's genetic advantage to stay with one female when he can get it on with several and pass more of his genes onto posterity. So males of most species either (1) try to accumulate harems, like gorillas; or (2) like orangutans, they scramble from female to female within their territories, reminiscent of the old traveling salesman making his rounds of the horny housewives.

For females, monogamy isn't so natural either. I know the old saying: "Hoggamus higgamus, man is polygamous. Higgamus hoggamus, woman's monogamous." Sounds good; but sorry, Jo, it just ain't so. Studies show that human females aren't much more monogamous than males, even though almost all societies punish women for cheating far more than men.

Nature bears this out. Females of many species prefer to live with female relatives and copulate with male visitors; lady elephants do this. If a female needs male protection, she travels in a mixed group and has sex with several males. That's what female chimps do, not to mention human swingers.

So how did monogamy evolve among humans? Very slowly. Basically, monogamy is the best policy when creatures like foxes, muskrats, and humans bear very helpless babies. Human babies are born so immature, they need constant supervision for at least four years.[1] Of course, some humans are so immature, they need constant supervision for forty years, but the minimum is four. Apparently, the monogamous human couple evolved to protect and take care of helpless infants. But—as we learned in Chemistry Class—according to nature, these couples didn't need to be permanent. Especially during our tempestuous reproductive years, humans were built to mate often and with different partners.

In addition to nature's pull, modern human relationships are bat-

---

[1]Fisher, *Anatomy of Love*, p. 153.

tered by the demands of child care, career, separate his and her work-
places, anxiety about paying the bills, geographical moves, a media
that glorifies the "new," a massive self-help movement that discourages couples from getting too dependent on each other, and a host of
other anti-love, anti-pleasure forces.

So how are we to stay together with
so much pulling us apart?

Most humans are sexual adventurers, sex being one of the great adventures in life, and find sex with only one person night after night,
year after year, to be tiresome, if not impossible. What they haven't
learned (and it does take some learning) is that monogamous sex can
be the greatest erotic adventure of all. Monogamy doesn't have to
equal monotony. It needn't be oppressive and tedious. It can be as
exciting as creating a great piece of art. Of course, art requires a bit
of work, and so does monogamy.

Monogamy is like a garden,
while natural human sexuality is like a jungle.

Gardens and jungles are both beautiful in their own ways. A jungle is wild and dangerous, untamed. A garden is safe and organized,
while still blooming with natural beauty. You don't need to cultivate
a jungle; it's natural. You do need to cultivate a garden, and most of
us do need to cultivate monogamy *if* we're going to enjoy it. But it's
not easy to cultivate a garden. Most gardens die. Most relationships—even those with love—lose their erotic luster. The commandments in this book teach you how to cultivate the garden of
monogamy, if that's what you want to do—that is, how to be a *sensual monogamist.*

To cultivate monogamy, you need total devotion.

I don't just mean being committed; that sounds like you've been
institutionalized! I mean being devoted—body and soul, heart,
brain, and gonads. As a monk or a nun is devoted to God, so you
must devote yourself to your primemate if you want to make
love last. And, of course, the really tricky part is finding someone you'd want to devote yourself to who also wants to be devoted to
you. I didn't say this was easy, just possible. And very much worthwhile.

A Note to Nonmonogamous Couples

Following these commandments is a tremendous aid to monogamy, but that's not to say that nonmonogamy can't be a legitimate lifestyle choice. Many "ethical hedonists" are nonmonogamous. Most people at the turn of the twenty-first century practice a sort of "serial monogamy," often with shades of bisexuality. If that's your situation, or if you're interested in swinging, triads, extended families, the *play-couple*[2] life, or other alternative lifestyles, these commandments will help you to give love and pleasure to your primemate as well as to the other ladies and gentlemen in your circle of playmates.

A Note to Same-Sex Couples

Just like lady/gentleman couples, whether you're in a gentleman/gentleman or lady/lady relationship, each of you has a male and a female side. Perhaps one of you is more obviously masculine or feminine than the other, maybe you switch back and forth, or maybe you're both just like sister-lovers or brother-primemates. Same-sex couples tend to be even more in touch with both their male and female sides, so I suggest you follow both sets of commandments for each other (with a few obvious exceptions, e.g., lesbians can pretty much skip Gentleman's Commandment #2: Thou Shalt Adore His Penis, though you may want to translate some of the material to "her clitoris," or perhaps "her strap-on"). If you have any questions, ask the expert, your primemate.

My advance apologies to same-sex couples for the fact that most of the pronoun usage in this book is geared toward the typical heterosexual couple consisting of one lady and one gentleman, but simplicity won out over political correctness here. It would have been rather unwieldy and tedious to try to address every possible sexual orientation under each commandment.

A Note to Unmarried Couples
Who Don't Know What to Call Each Other

If you aren't married and you don't know what to call your better half when introducing him or her to friends or family ("better half"

[2]Term coined by Dr. Robert McGinley of the Lifestyles Organization, to mean couples who explore sensual pleasures with other couples.

sounds sort of silly, "partner" sounds so businesslike, "lover" sounds sleazy, "roommate" sounds too casual), why not introduce him or her as your "primemate"? It's primal, loving, exclusive, has a certain bonobo panache, and should get a very interesting conversation going. I'm sure you've noticed by now that I use this term quite a bit. Max and I started referring to each other as "my primemate" after we learned about the bonobos, even though bonobos are definitely not monogamous, and we are.

A Note to Single People

Just because I keep talking about "your primemate" doesn't mean you must have one to benefit from following these commandments. Though much of what they offer focuses on two people in a long-term relationship, a lot of material deals with dating. If you're looking for a primemate of your own, they will help you find, attract, and hold on to someone worthy of you. If you'd rather make like an orangutan and "play the field," following them will increase your likelihood of "scoring" with the ladies and/or gentlemen who interest you. If you're looking for someone who will follow these commandments *for you,* you could place a personal ad for a "primemate."[3] Or just give this book as a gift on your next date.

By the way, just because you don't currently have a primemate doesn't mean you can't give erotic pleasure to someone special. If you're by yourself, give yourself pleasure. It's important that somebody do it—after all, nature didn't intend for human beings to live alone and uncuddled! So, if you happen to be a product of modern desocialization, living alone, all by yourself, take care of yourself: Take a bubblebath, rub your feet with scented oil, read an erotic story, masturbate, love yourself. I know it's much better when someone else does all that with you, but as that troubadour of the 1970s, Stephen Stills, used to sing: "If you can't be with the one you love, love the one you're with." *Love your sweet lovable self.* It sounds corny, but it's true: Loving, respecting, taking care of, and giving pleasure to yourself is an important part of getting you in shape for doing all of that for someone else.

[3]For more on personal ads, check out my first book: *Advertising for Love* (New York: William Morrow, 1984).

Notes on "Safe Sex"
Sex can be dangerous—though not as dangerous as walking the streets at night, or even driving some streets in broad daylight! But safe sex is very important. And safe sex is more than just spermicidal latex slipcovers; safe sex is phone sex, massage, mutual masturbation, light spanking, reciprocal caressing, holding hands, dancing close, your bodies snaking around each other. I know it's not necessarily *as* pleasurable as the so-called real thing. But you don't always have to have *maximum pleasure,* as long as you have some pleasure. Always take your time with sex, and try to enjoy the time you take.

To avoid adding paragraphs of material about latex and spermicide to every other commandment, I've assumed that the ladies and gentlemen participating in all acts involving an exchange of body fluids are either in a strictly monogamous relationship, or else they are adapting safer sex techniques and accessories to the activity at hand (or mouth, as the case may be).

If you have any doubt about your health or your partner's health, practice some form of safer sex. Avoid the exchange of body fluids, especially blood and semen. Use spermicidal jelly, latex condoms, and dental dams, but don't stop there. Use your erotic imagination to come up with ways to "make love" that don't involve an exchange of body fluids. Try the aforementioned safer sex shenanigans or dry humping (sex with clothes on), extragenital stimulation or "outercourse" (erotic play with feet, hands, ears, and other nongenital body parts), and whatever else you can dream up that shares sexual pleasure without sharing sexual germs.

Save Sex
That said, keep this in mind: AIDS is *not* retribution for the "sins" of the sexual revolution. Unprotected, full-blown sexual intercourse with different people has always been dangerous. Life is dangerous, and sex is the essence of life.[4] With AIDS, sex can kill you. Until not so long ago, sex could always kill you. For much of human history,

---

[4]Food, another "essence of life," is also dangerous. Consider how many people get sick and die from bad food, whether it's instant food poisoning or a slower death of heart disease from living on a junk food diet.

syphilis was usually as deadly as it was common, and childbirth was extremely hazardous.

Practice safe sex, but don't use fear of AIDS as an excuse for your own sexophobia, homophobia, or heterophobia. Just because we live in the age of AIDS doesn't mean sex is the root of all evil. Sex is the root of life, and life sometimes begets death through sex, though not very often. *Sex begets life far more often than death.* All kinds of life.

Safe sex is important, always has been, always will be. But *saving sex* is even more important because it heals a billion times more than it kills.

Notes on Mixing Business with Pleasure

I believe in mixing business with pleasure, especially when work takes up a lot of your life. One way to get pleasure out of work is to *give* pleasure at work, to those you work with. If you are so inclined, you can use these commandments (obviously, adaptations are necessary) to enhance your popularity with coworkers, employees, and, of course, the boss. For that matter, you can use them to establish better relations with everyone in your life, from your in-laws to your gardener.

Please don't take this the wrong way. I'm not suggesting that you have love affairs with your boss, your in-laws, or your gardener (though if you already are, you'll want to follow these commandments so at least you'll be a lady or gentleman about it). As you'll discover, there is much within these commandments that applies to situations and relationships that are not overtly sexual.

Notes on Language

Talk is cheap—and very, very valuable. The foundation of a great sex life is good communication. Since human beings are, to a great extent, verbal creatures, that means talking. When people can talk about their sexual interests and desires, as well as their fears and insecurities, they create an environment that is conducive to giving and receiving pleasure. Unfortunately, because of society's longstanding repressive attitude toward sex, even the most articulate of us can get tongue-tied when talking about the simplest sexual subjects.

Sex is not easy to speak about.

On radio, TV, and at my Institute, I host "Speakeasies" where I try to help people to find a vocabulary with which to *speak* about sex that is neither too vulgar nor overly clinical, but intelligent, erotic, empathetic, good-humored, and, though not always easy, at least understandable.

In many circles, sex is virtually unspeakable.

Of course, *speaking* includes vocal inflection that helps to communicate the meaning of words that are not adequate in and of themselves. Unfortunately, aside from the right to use italics or exclamation points every so often, I can't use the helpful tool of vocal inflection in writing this book. So I am dependent on the rather sex-negative vagaries of the English language itself.

Over my years of trying to communicate about sex through speaking and writing, I've come to realize that there are no "good" words for certain sexual acts, feelings, and body parts. The ultimate sex act itself is probably the most difficult to name. The polite term *intercourse* is so antiseptic that it is also the name of a famously prudish Amish town in Lancaster, Pennsylvania. The technical terms *coitus, coition,* and *copulation* sound like something you do in a lab with monitoring devices attached to your genitals. The biblical term *fornication* sounds like something only goats and heathens do. The romantic term *make love* is all right, but too laden with emotional meaning for many uses. And the slang term *fuck* is considered one of the coarsest, rudest words in the English language, and is most often used to mean things that have nothing to do with the sharing of sexual pleasure.

Then there are the body parts that can barely be named in any dialect without setting off gasps or giggles. In writing this book, I've chosen to alternate the use of clinical words like *penis* and *vulva* with nonderogatory slang terms like *cock* and *pussy.* In using the slang, I don't wish to offend anyone or cheapen the message. But in certain contexts, I feel that the clinical words don't convey feelings of pleasure or excitement as effectively as slang terms (unless you're into doctor or nurse fantasies).

The Pleasure Point System

You're almost ready for the commandments! But first, you need a basic understanding of my "Pleasure Point System." If you know anything about acupressure massage, you know that you have "pressure points" all over your body. These are points you can press or penetrate for the purpose of healing. There are also what I call "pleasure points" all over our bodies and in our minds. The commandments in this book guide you in how to find, "press," and "penetrate" the common and unique pleasure points of anyone you wish to pleasure.

Pleasure points are like pressure points—
activating them gives pleasure.

My Pleasure Point System is not very complicated. It's just a way of discovering and handling emotional and physical "hot spots." For example, you might have a pleasure point in your big toe that loves to be sucked, or in your rear end which adores being spanked, or in your mind which craves hearing whispers of passion or pledges of devotion or intense, orgiastic fantasies.

Your pleasure points change, of course, depending upon the time of day or time of life. If you're a lady, they also change with the time of month. But they're always there, these little erotic entryways through our armor that allow us to receive pleasure. Why do we wear the armor, hiding our pleasure points, even from ourselves? Because many pleasure points are also points of pain, points of fear, guilt, and shame. The road to pleasure leads through a minefield—you never know when you're going to step on something explosive!

Each of us has a different erotic nature, a complex quilt of many influences, including what's in our genes and how we fill out our jeans, our cultural background, the events of our childhood and adolescence, along with more recent adult experiences. Thus, our pleasure points are all placed a bit differently. So, there is no one "answer" to the question of how to give a lady or gentleman pleasure, and anyone who tells you they have *the* answer is full of how-to horsepuckey.

There is only exploration, point by personal pleasure point.

To some degree, you can use your instincts to find your primemate's personal pleasure points and to touch them without causing pain. But you shouldn't expect to pick all this up by instinct alone. Ask lots of questions, and pay attention to the answers. The following commandments are here to help you to ask the right questions, both verbally and nonverbally, and to deal with the responses. They will also help sharpen your instincts.

Now turn the page into paradise . . .

The

10

COMMANDMENTS

of a

LADY'S

PLEASURE

I

THOU SHALT

Pay Attention to the Details

of Her Desire

Her Holy Grail

Imagine that you are a gentleman, a modern knight of great honor, courage, and gentility, on a quest for the Holy Grail.[1]

In the times of the troubadours, the "Holy Grail" was a very special symbol of the power of love. While most symbols of power in those days were swords, the Grail was *not* a weapon but a sacred cup that gave the knight who held it tremendous power. The Grail you seek is another special symbolic cup: it holds the love of your lady.

You must follow the path of her pleasure points to win
the cup that overflows with her love.

This is not an easy path to follow, either in the songs of the medieval troubadours or in the modern search for a lady's pleasures. Like any difficult but worthy path, it requires your full attention. It is thick with the thorny brambles of her sexual psyche, her hopes and fears, fantasies and nightmares. Her pleasure points are also points of

---

[1]For a different, but very illuminating psychological interpretation of how the myth of the Holy Grail deals with a man's struggle to "find himself" and come to terms with his own inner feminine side, see Robert A. Johnson's classic book, *He: Understanding Masculine Psychology* (New York: Harper & Row, 1977).

pain, after all. Clouds of sociosexual repression obscure the view. Wild creatures from her past may leap across the path or attack you. But if you are the gentleman *for her,* the gentleman who can give her pleasure, you will do whatever it takes to move through these obstacles and get to her Holy Grail. Use these commandments as a map.

Horny Housewives

Many of my male clients and callers ask me how to "turn on" a woman (as though she's a TV set!), and the best single piece of advice I can give them is this: Pay attention. They're always quick to claim that they *do* pay attention, but after a bit of mild interrogation, I usually find that they don't.

They tend to start out by complaining that their wives refuse to have sex with them, and accuse them of being horny perverts for wanting it.

Are all these ladies really such cold, sexless bitches?

Dave, an executive, married sixteen years, two teenage kids, has what he calls "boring sex" with his wife for ten minutes about once every two weeks. He says she doesn't want to do it more often, and doesn't even seem to like doing it *that* much. Meanwhile, Dave is having elaborate sexual fantasies of getting dressed up, tied up, plugged up, spanked, licked, sucked, and tickled, but when he tries to get his wife to get into doing all this stuff, she just says *no way.*

"Why not?" I ask.

"She's not interested in sex," he says.

Why isn't she interested? Dave doesn't know. He just keeps insisting that his wife is not interested in sex and he is. But sex is not something like golf or bird-watching that some people are interested in and some people are not. We are all sexual beings, and, essentially, though sometimes subconsciously, we are all interested in sex. However, we have different personalities and backgrounds, *different details to our desires,* and we're *not* all interested in the same *kind* of sex.

Certainly, we're not all interested in the kind of sex Dave wants.

So, I ask simple things like "What kind of sex is your wife interested in?" Well, guess what? Dave has no idea. I go down a list of things he can do to get her to let him know what kinds of sexual pleasures she might enjoy—mostly simple things, like "ask her"—but Dave hasn't thought of any of them. He's too busy thinking about what turns him on. It's nice that Dave is so aware of the details of *his* desires, but if he's going to have a fulfilling sex life with his wife, *he has to pay attention to the details of* her *desires, too.*

Men like Dave assume they're much hornier than their wives, but they have no idea how horny their wives would be if they could have the kind of sex that really turns *them* on.

Could You Be Dave?

If I were Dave's wife, and if for sixteen years we only had sex according to *his* desires, and *never mine*, I wouldn't be so horny, either. I'm sure I would wind up loathing that awful little ten-minute once-every-two-weeks hump session. And, unless I was having an affair with someone who cared about the details of my desires, I would probably go sexually numb.

Which is what happens to a lot of ladies. Their sexuality is so repressed and denigrated, censored and belittled, ignored and abused, that they just stop feeling sexual. They channel all their erotic feelings into more "acceptable" pursuits, such as their children (a classic sublimation object for a sexually frustrated woman's erotic feelings that can, of course, *really* screw up the kids!), their work, their hobbies, their gardening, their aerobics classes, their compulsive shopping, their drinking binges, their eating disorders.

Do you want your lady to be a great "horny housewife"—or horny corporate president or horny neurosurgeon? Do you want her to channel at least part of her sex drive into sex? Then you must honor her female sexual nature, discover the pleasure points throughout her body and mind, share her fantasies, partake in her deepest, darkest sexual psychodramas, and *pay attention to the details of her desire*.

It is a difficult quest. As American writer Irma Kurtz said, "It would be less demanding, enslaving, perplexing, and strenuous for a healthy male to screw a thousand women in his lifetime than to try to please one, and the potential for failure would be less."[2] Yet nothing is more fulfilling.

[2]Irma Kurtz, *Mantalk: A Book for Women Only* (New York: William Morrow, 1987).

Pay attention to the words of that most romantic of English novelists, D. H. Lawrence:

> *The greatest living experience for every man*
> *is his adventure into the woman.*[3]

Keep that thought close to your heart as you strive to follow these 10 Commandments of a Lady's Pleasure in your quest for her Holy Grail.

What If She Says She Just Wants to Please You?

What if you ask her what she likes, and she says, "Whatever *you* like"? Keep asking.

There is no creature alive whose only *pleasure is to please others.*

But since society so strongly condemns the expression of female erotic pleasure, ladies are far more reticent about broadcasting their desires than gentlemen. That doesn't mean they don't have them.

Recently, I interviewed several young women for a TV show about female pleasure. At first, they claimed that the only thing that gave them pleasure was to please someone else. "Fine," I said, "but what if that someone else wants to give *you* pleasure? What should that person do?" At first, these young ladies literally couldn't answer. They giggled, hemmed and hawed, went off on tangents, and kept coming back to "whatever you like" types of answers. But with relentless yet gentle and rather seductive probing, the answers poured forth like the proverbial water out of the dike: "Rub my feet . . . Do my dishes . . . Hold me . . . Pay my bills . . . Tongue my ear . . . Help me with my career . . . Kiss me softly . . . Suck my clit . . . Earrings, I love earrings . . . Respect me . . . Worship my body . . . Spank me . . . Massage my shoulders . . . Do my taxes . . . Cook for me . . . Cuddle me . . . Drive me around on a Harley . . . Caress my breasts . . . Take me to Paris . . . Love me unconditionally. . . ."

Of course, they got tremendous pleasure out of just *revealing* the

[3]D. H. Lawrence letter to Bertrand Russell, February 24, 1915, published in *The Letters of D. H. Lawrence.* Vol. 2, George J. Zytaruk and James T. Boulton, eds. (New York: Cambridge University Press, 1979).

true details of their desires to someone who genuinely wanted to know. Speaking of which, Thou Shalt Pay Attention to the Details of Her Desire doesn't mean you actually have to *grant* all of her desires; just deal with them, take them seriously. The ladies on that TV show were pleased as pleasantly spiked punch just to have their real desires paid attention to.

Do the Dishes, Rub Her Feet

Feminine mystery is exciting. But the way to give the lady pleasure is to get past her mysteries and discover the details of her personal realities, however mundane. It's ironic that the way to a sexy lady's heart and genitals may be to do the dishes and rub her feet, but sometimes it's the truth!

Back to School

What if you're incredibly selfish and not really interested in *her* desires, let alone their details? You still ought to follow this commandment. Think of it as fair play. That is, if you want your lady to be more interested in or at least tolerant of *your* desires, your best bet is to pay very close attention to hers. She may be easy; you might be able to get away with just caressing her breasts and paying her bills. Then, again, she may require unconditional love and a trip to Paris.

If you are "attention span–impaired," think of it this way: Your lady is the sexiest schoolteacher you've ever had. Even if you're more experienced than her, you have a lot to learn about the details of her unique sexuality. She is the only one who can teach you those details. *And you will be tested.*

Now are you paying attention?

Another Good Reason to Give a Lady Pleasure

Not only is all this a pleasure for her and a thrill for you, it's good for society. As the social evolutionist Riane Eisler points out, "Be they secular or religious, Christian or Muslim, ancient or modern, Eastern or Western, the times and places where we find the greatest sexual repression of women are generally also the times and places where political repression is most severe."[4] Conversely, when ladies are sexually the freest, so is everyone.

[4]Riane T. Eisler, *Sacred Pleasure* (New York: HarperCollins, 1995), p. 214.

The research of developmental neuropsychologist James Prescott, who studied violent behavior and sex in forty-nine cultures, backs this up. Prescott found that "the greater the sexual restrictions on the female, the greater is the violence of that culture."[5] All in all, it looks like paying attention to the details of a lady's desire is not *just* about having a good time, it's also about keeping the peace. It is one of the basic principles of the Bonobo Way.

A Society of Ignoramuses in the Realm of Female Sexual Desire

Thanks to both nature and nurture, the male tends to become aroused more quickly and easily than the female, i.e., he gets hornier faster. This makes it difficult for the average gentleman to comprehend fully how *many* details a lady needs taken care of before she can even feel her desires.

Don't feel too bad if, at this point, you "just don't get it." There are very few societies in which men are actually taught to give women pleasure. In *our* society, most men aren't even taught how to have sex, much less how to discover the details of female sexual desire. They are just expected to "know" these things. They don't.

Over the past decade, I've talked privately and publicly with thousands of men about sex, and I am sincerely sorry to report that most men are total ignoramuses about female sexual desire. Many think they know all about female pleasure, assuming it is the same as male, or else taking for granted that it is the opposite. Either attitude can be disastrous.

If you *know* how to touch a woman's pleasure points, you can turn her on, you can even heal her pain. If you *don't*, you'll most likely just make her sick.

What's the Fuss?
The human female loves sex as much as the male. It's not always true that "men want it and women have it," but we could say that the

---

[5]Lyn Ehrnstein, "A Brain-Mind Theory of Culture, Sexuality and Moral Behavior: An Interview with Dr. James Prescott," *Floodtide*. Vol. 3, no. 4 (Summer 1992), p. 2.

male tends to want "it" more often and *with less fuss*. The female loves to be fussed over. The medieval troubadours worshipped and served the ladies they adored. No amount of fuss was too much. Ladies eat that up.

Make Her Choose You

The medieval troubadours sang of ladies who *chose* the gentlemen they *desired*. This was quite a revolutionary statement during a time when women were often raped by men, and girls were usually "given away" in marriage by their fathers, with no choice at all on the part of the female. A smart gentleman learned that paying attention to the details of his fair lady's desire would win him her love. In modern times, as in nature, most females do the choosing in the mating game.[6]

Pay attention to your lady, and she'll choose you every time.

Safety Before Pleasure

A gentleman protects a lady. It sounds corny, and some feminists will bark at me, but the female needs to feel safe to feel pleasure. Her pleasure requires a foundation of comfort and support.

The window to her deep desires opens
only to the extent that she feels safe.

This stuff was second nature to the troubadours, but modern gentlemen courting strong career women often forget this vital detail. Don't be chauvinist; do be chivalrous.

Support your female primemate by helping her take care of the details of her *life* before you even get to the details of her desire (see Lady's Commandment #7: Thou Shalt Give Her Things, page 49). The female is said to be the more romantic gender, but she can be very practical when it comes to sex. Some women can't relax if the carpet needs vacuuming, but they're too tired to do it. Vacuuming the carpet (or giving the baby a bath or helping her prepare for her morning meeting or whatever needs doing) can be great foreplay for an overworked, overwhelmed woman.

[6]Check out Mary Batten's book, *Sexual Strategies: How Females Choose Their Mates* (New York: Putnam Publishing Group, 1992), for more on how in most species, the female seems to choose the male.

Honestly, feeling relieved and grateful can turn to feeling horny!

Female practicality stems from nurture as well as nature. Since society discourages women from taking pure pleasure in sex, ladies tend to become practical about it. Also, because women can get pregnant and are more susceptible to contracting most sexually transmitted diseases, if they value their lives, they *have* to be practical.

Of course, when it comes to sex, the ultimate practical female is the "golddigger." Don't go overboard in catering to her practical needs, unless you're already in a serious relationship, or you may find yourself being used.

Love Is Her Favorite Fetish

The female must feel loved and cared for to enjoy pleasure. Most women are very involved in caring for and pleasing others. This pulls them away from the details of their own desires. When a lady is temporarily released from her duties to others, she can start to feel her desire for pleasure.

To feel pleasure, the female needs to feel loved.

A man might say, "We have to *make* love before we can have love." But most ladies need to *feel* loved, or at least the possibility of being loved, before they will joyously *make* love.

Think Fast . . . Go Slow

Arousal tends to build slowly in the female, giving you plenty of time to pay attention to the details of her desire. Don't let your hormonal impatience blow it for you. As the nineteenth-century Danish philosopher Søren Kierkegaard pointed out, "Most men pursue pleasure with such breathless haste that they hurry past it."[7] Take advantage of the time that she needs. And remember:

The best-laid plans may not get you laid the way you planned!

Don't blow your cool over this. After all, this isn't about getting *you* laid; it's about giving *her* pleasure (hopefully, for both your sakes, the

---

[7]Søren Kierkegaard, *Either/Or*. Vol. 1, "Diapsalmata" (1843).

two coincide fairly often). But the female is unpredictable. So, stay loose. Be flexible. Be a gentleman.

No Cheating

If you stray from the path of your lady's pleasure to dally on other paths, you will get *lost* before you find her Holy Grail. When you cheat on her, even if she never finds out, you not only lose her trust, you divert your attention away from her, draining her potential for pleasure. Swinging and open relationships are a different matter (see Gentleman's Commandment #5: Thou Shalt Excite Him, page 123).

Be a Master Pleasure-Giver

To follow this commandment fully, to really *pay attention to the details of her desire,* a gentleman needs to get in touch with his feminine side, what the Taoists call his "yin" energy, what Jung called his "anima." This may be disturbing for you. Paying attention to the details of anything is usually considered "women's work." Many men in our society are raised to feel contempt for women's work and so-called effeminate emotions like "caring" and "fussing." All I can say to these men is: Get over it!

Paying attention to the details won't make you less of a man.

It will make you a *gentle* man. And it will make you a master pleasure-giver.

As you discover her personal details, you should also attend to her common female pleasure points. You'll find them in the rest of these commandments.

Recommended Reading

French, Marilyn. *The Women's Room.* New York: Summit Books, 1977.

Harding, M. Esther. *The Way of All Women.* New York: G. P. Putnam's Sons, 1970.

Johnson, Robert. *She: Understanding Feminine Psychology.* New York: Harper & Row, 1976.

2

THOU SHALT

Stimulate Her Senses

The Sensuality of Sex

Sexual pleasure is sensual. We perceive and receive pleasure through our eyes, ears, nostrils, the tips of our tongues, and the surfaces of our skin. No matter how much we might romanticize or intellectualize erotic pleasure, we cannot connect with it, except through our five senses.

> *To give a lady pleasure, help her to relax her defenses*
> *and wake up her senses.*

And make sure to provide something gorgeous, mellifluous, and delicious for her to wake up to!

Visual Attraction
Whether it's due to the nature of men or the nurture of boys, most guys, especially very young or very horny guys, can get turned on by simply *looking* at an attractive lady. There are exceptions, but generally, the female tends not to be *so* visual, and though ultimately women are just as horny as men are, the female is not so easily or instantly aroused. Of course, looks make a big impression on almost everybody, and the woman of the twenty-first century often wants

her man to primp for her. For more information on how to use your looks to give your female or male primemate pleasure, see Gentleman's Commandment #3: Thou Shalt Be a Source of Beauty in His Life (page 110).

Music of the Spheres for Her Sensitive Ears

It's more vital that you *say* things to turn the female on, that you speak intimately, confidently, humorously, romantically, and, of course, personally. "A man falls in love through his eyes," said British writer Woodrow Wyatt, "a woman through her ears." Most ladies are lovers of sweet sentences.

Entice her into aural sex. Tell her you want her, you crave her, you love her passionately. Tell her stories. Find out her dreams and fantasies, and murmur them into her ear as you make love. We humans are animals in many ways, especially when it comes to sex. But unlike animals, we have an ability to communicate complex ideas and images through speech. Take advantage of this uniquely human talent, and say the words she needs to hear. But don't lie, darling!

Thou shalt not bear false witness against thy neighbor.[1]

Remember to practice *ethical* hedonism.

Animals do have mating calls. Make special sounds that let her know you want to pleasure her. They can be soft and sexy or strong and manly or endearingly silly. Max grunts like a bonobo chimp when he wants to go down on me, then moans and coos and tells me I'm delicious as he slurps away. That always makes me feel like sucking his banana.

If you have no idea what to say, just say her name. Real or pet names will do. Whisper it, savor it, sing it out as you come to her. . . .

Play Music Man

Partly because of the female lust for auditory stimulation, ladies love musicians. If you can't play an instrument (air guitar doesn't count), at least learn to be a decent DJ. Play music to suit her moods, her

---

[1] Just in case you don't know your original Ten Commandments, this one's number nine.

sense of sound. Let the music leave your instrument, or stereo system, and blaze a trail to her Holy Grail right through her ears.

Wake Up and Smell the Sex!

Since our culture emphasizes our sense of sight and sound so much, most of us give short shrift to our sense of smell. But it's vital, especially when it comes to sex, where our olfactory sense can work in mysterious ways. For instance, have you ever found yourself inexplicably attracted to someone who's not at all your physical or mental type? It could very well be that you're being seduced by the way that person smells. Likewise, you can be totally turned off by an otherwise nice, attractive person for no other reason but that they smell like something growing at the bottom of an abandoned refrigerator.

> *Animals sniff each other during courtship.*
> *So does the human female.*

Smells are part of what makes up that mystical thing we call *chemistry*, even part of that mystical thing we call *love*. People put so much stock in how others look, we sometimes forget how important the scent of someone is. Until we get up close . . .

Thou Shalt Shower
The human female tends to be more sensitive to odor than the male. So make sure you *smell* good. *Some* ladies might like a man who smells like a buffalo emerging from a sweat lodge, but most do not. One of my sex therapy clients couldn't understand why his wife of six months loathed sex with him, even though she'd loved it when they were dating. After a few questions, I discovered that since they'd gotten married, he'd changed his showering habits, taking a shower *after* he got out of bed with her instead of *before* getting into bed with her like he did when they were in courting mode. When he reversed the pattern, lo and behold, she got interested in sex again! Just a little detail, but it's all in the details, darling.

Don't forget to wash behind your balls, brush your teeth, and clean between your tushcakes! Those who haven't seen a bar of soap since the fall of the Berlin Wall might want to visit the local car wash.

Whether it's due to testosterone, hyperactivity, or a lot of beer, the human male does have a greater tendency to stink than the female. Only one part of a lady is perceived to be as smelly, her vagina, whereas there are many more parts of a gentleman which, when unscrubbed, tend to emit noxious fumes.

Eau de Josephine

Furthermore, the human male tends not to be so sensitive to smell. Remember what Napoleon wrote to Josephine: "I'll be arriving in Paris tomorrow. Don't bathe." He adored her naturally strong, female odor. We don't know exactly how Josephine felt about Napoleon's unwashed bouquet, but she probably bustled him into the bath—or at least, the bidet—as soon as he came home. Of course, nobody washed much in those days. Most of those elegant, beautiful Parisians probably stunk like billy goats.

The Smell of Leather

Choose your cologne as carefully as you choose your clothes, as your scent reveals something special about your personality and style. Light perfumes convey freshness and innocence while musky, woodsy colognes are darker and more boldly sensual. Spicy aromas send a message of exotic unpredictability. Summer roses might arouse a memory of young love; the smell of leather may stir fantasies of domination and surrender. One reason that people who are into bondage, dominance, and submission are into leather is that they're turned on by its powerful animal *odor*. I love it, maybe because the first boy I ever French-kissed when I was fourteen years old was wearing a leather jacket. Speaking of smells, his breath smelled terrible—a rather potent mixture of Budweiser and filterless Chesterfields—especially for a Colgate-mouthed kid like me. But his *jacket* smelled delicious, and that's probably what kept me making out with him for hours that night.

Breath: The Vital Vapor of Life (and Sex)

Help to enhance her sense of smell by encouraging her to relax, receive, and breathe slowly and deeply from her belly, before, during, or after sex. Slow, deep breathing will open her senses and lower her blood pressure, increasing the likelihood of arousal and orgasm. For more on the orgasmic power of deep breathing, see Gentleman's Commandment #4: Thou Shalt Inspire Him (page 116).

Be Aroma-Friendly

Garlic is a traditional aphrodisiac. And it does clear the sinuses and open the senses! But if you eat it, make sure your primemate does, too. In general, you are most "aroma-compatible" when you eat the same foods and exude the same scents. Same goes for libations. If you're drinking alcohol, and she's not, you'll smell (to her) like a brewery.

If you please your primemate's olfactory sense, you may find that she almost literally inhales you! And if she genuinely likes your natural aroma, you have a good chance at everlasting love.

Questions of Taste

The tongue, the tastemeister, is one of the most erotic, excitable, exploratory parts of the human body. Your tongue is very much like a genital organ. It's very sensitive, especially the tip of your tongue, and it's always very wet. People who are naturally oral instinctively love to taste, to lick, to put just about anything into their mouths. The female tends to adore tasting, eating, licking, nibbling, sucking, savoring, devouring, biting, kissing. . . . After all, what is kissing but two people tasting each other?

The Joy of Kissing

> "Let him kiss me with the kisses of his mouth:
> for thy love is better than wine."[2]

Ladies loves to kiss. The smart female can tell how a gentleman will make love by the way he kisses. As the great risqué entertainer Mae West noted, "A man's kiss is his signature." So brush up on your tongue play. When in doubt, start light and soft. Tease and play before you get into any deep passionate plunging. Pay attention to her lips. Use her tongue as your guide.

Now, you might think that sexually speaking, kissing—even French kissing—is pretty tame stuff. And on a certain level, that's true. People can kiss with all their clothes on. They can kiss in pub-

---

[2] The Song of Songs 1:2 (between Job and Ruth in your Bible).

lic, and it's no big deal. Kissing is not exactly a rare, hot, exotic, kinky, sexual experience in most of our adult lives. Or is it? Or, should I say, can it be? Can it be the rarest, hottest, most exotic, kinky, intimate, intense, delicious sexual experience of all? It *can* . . . can't it?

> *Haven't you ever had one of* those *kisses? Where you start to feel the aura of erotic heat hovering around your mouth before your lover's lips even touch yours. . . . Then you look into each other's eyes hungrily, then your hands are in each other's hair, your bodies move in sync, and your lips touch, brush, so lightly, sweetly, and softly at first . . . . You feel the warmth, the life, the energy, through your lips, your face, your throat, your bloodstream, circling to a central point of passionate intensity right between your legs, whirling around your body, down deep into your soul and then back through your lips, pushing them harder and more urgently against each other, with your tongues waiting, poised within your mouths, like trained seals anticipating the moment when they leap out of their cages, past your teeth, your lips, and into a wild wet dance in each other's mouths—two trained seals, flying fish, nymphs of the saliva sea . . . sucking on the nectar of love . . . tasting it, licking it, biting it, savoring it, swallowing it, slurping it, kissing it.*

At this point, such kissing either turns into something more serious, or it just turns into more kissing, depending on what the lady wants to do. *You're* giving *her* pleasure, right? If she wants to keep it on the safe-sex, makeout level, kissing like this can go on and on and on, standing up, lying down, swinging on the porch swing, standing under a waterfall, sitting in a convertible with the top down on a starry night, standing in the middle of a city sidewalk during lunch hour while hundreds of people rush by (though I'm sure a few would stop and watch you). Kissing, even deep, wet tongue kissing, is extremely portable. It's an incredibly erotic act you can indulge in just about anywhere. And it can be quick. It's not just safe sex, it's *instant* sex, which can be important in these high-speed times. Kisses can be like vitamins, providing emotional nutrients, maybe even chemical ones. So, listen to your doctor: Take at least eight pecks and four French kisses a day, and call me in the morning.

By the way, smart gentlemen shave before bed. The unshaven look may be trendy, but it's not very kissable.

The Importance of Tasting Good . . .

. . . especially if you want your fair lady to swallow. The taste of a man's semen, like the taste and smell of other body excretions, has a lot to do with what you eat (see Gentleman's Commandment #10: Thou Shalt Swallow, page 167). Stay away from asparagus before sex. It makes your urine smell rancid and can make your semen taste almost as bad. Drink lots of water to clean yourself out. I've heard from several old wives and a few young chippies that the taste of a man's semen improves when he eats celery. No, it doesn't make your semen taste like celery! It just makes it taste fresh and nice (partly because celery has so much water). And don't you want to taste fresh and nice? Of course you do. So start chomping that rabbit food, boys, and ladies will love the taste of your sperm! Also, try pineapple juice, kiwi, and anything flavored with cinnamon. Cinnamon is the sex spice. I should write a cookbook next, huh?

Dr. Block's Recipes for Sweet-Tastin' Semen
(with long-lasting results)

Celery with cayenne pepper
add a little vodka and tomato juice
and you've got a hard-driving, sperm-sweetening Bloody Mary!

Pineapple juice with a cinnamon stick

Cinnamon-spiced kiwi-pineapple fruit compôte

Juicy Fingers

Your primemate may enjoy the taste of her own juices. If she's not into it, don't push her, but if she is, after you finger her, bring your vaginal-juice-soaked fingers up to her nose and mouth. Let her sniff and suck her wetness as a gift from her to you, and back to her. After you've been sucking her, let her kiss her own musky honey off your lips and cheeks.

Culinary Aphrodisiacs

The female loves to combine food and sex, two of the most vital elements of the continuity of life, two of the richest representations of love. Why do you think those candlelight dinners have become such a romantic cliché? There are, of course, kinkier ways to combine food and sex. Plan an evening of wanton sensual carnality. Pour something delicious—chocolate sauce, whipped cream, caviar, Grand Marnier—into an intimate orifice or spread it on a delectable surface of her body, then slowly slurp it off. Or let her slurp you. Max sticks shrimps between my toes, dabs a little cocktail sauce on the ball of my foot, and gobbles me up into a toegasmic frenzy.

Keeping in Touch

What is the female's largest sexual organ? Her skin. There's a lot to touch—so many curves and bends and silky plains. Revel in the luscious glory of her flesh as you caress and squeeze and spank and embrace her. You can reach the depths of her soul through touching the surface of her skin.

The pleasure of touch is so powerful. It can relieve stress, sometimes even cure illnesses. Touch can seal deals with a handshake, bond friendships with a nice warm hug, and turn strangers into lovers with a single electrifying stroke. Touch can also be terrible; violence is a form of touch. But one reason that people are violent is that they don't get touched enough in positive, healing, and yes, sexual, ways. People need touch so badly, they'll get it any way they can. If they can't get touch that is pleasurable, they may well take or give touch that is painful.

Touch can communicate many feelings—affection, power, desire. Conventional wisdom is that men use touch to get sex, and women use sex to get touch. But *everybody needs to be touched.* Studies have shown that infants get sick and die from nothing but a lack of touch.

The joy of touch isn't just touchy-feely talk. It's biochemical. Certain kinds of touch create a feeling of euphoria, stimulating the release of beta endorphins that are chemically similar to opium. In other words, touch gives you drug-free ecstasy. Now let's learn how to cultivate that ecstasy.

Ways to Touch Her

Cuddle Up
The female is very sensitive to touch. Her body craves it, but tends not to like to be touched too intimately too fast, especially when she doesn't know you well. Even if she does know you and love you, when she's had a stressful day or even if she's just in a don't-touch-me-too-fast-down-there mood, she can be skittish. As cute and flattering as having her breasts and genitals pawed and grabbed might be, it just won't do it for her sexually. It's not that she doesn't like being touched genitally, she loves it! The female even loves to be *pawed* and, of course, penetrated, at a certain point. She even enjoys being "manhandled." The key word here is: foreplay. Best to build slowly, teasingly, *before* any passionate pawing or manhandling. When in doubt, cuddle. The female adores being cuddled. She can fall in head-over-spiked-high-heels love with you on the basis of cuddling alone. Being cuddled makes her feel girlish, safe, comfy, cherished, and very, very close to you. In fact, a subcommandment here should be: Thou Shalt Cuddle.

Somewhere between pure love and hot sex lies sweet affection. *Cuddling is affection in action.*

Sensual Massage
The female loves massage. The male likes it, too, but the female *loves* it. Many a night, a lady will say (and sincerely believe) that she is not in the mood for sex, but she will gladly give her body up to a good massage, and that is very likely to put her in the mood for sex.

Learn the art of massage, if you don't already know it. Massage her back, feet, thighs, arms, hands, shoulders, tummy, breasts, and buns in a way that is at first *not* explicitly sexual, then by degrees increasingly erotic. Playfully brush by her clit as if by accident in the course of the massage, then gradually get more deliberate. Tease her with your touch. Everybody needs to be teased.

> *The male needs to be teased because it makes him slow down.*
> *The female needs to be teased because it makes her come around.*

As you touch her teasingly, indirectly, stroking or rubbing and then pulling away, she will come around to wanting you to touch her more. Touch her in places where she is not usually touched, places that are not considered "sexual," like her neck, her shoulders, the in-sides of her elbows.

Touch her genitals in different, less obviously sexual ways. For in-stance, cover her entire vulva with your hand and just hold it there, pressing down slowly and firmly. The pressure feels very comforting and arousing at the same time. It's very simple, most ladies love it, and few gentlemen do it.

Remember, when in doubt, go slow and steady.

A fast, nervous touch is more annoying to the female than a fly on her nose!

Try to move with her breathing. Help her to breathe deep and open her senses by breathing deeply yourself. Deep breathing can be contagious. Start by breathing in sync with her, gradually deepen your breathing, and she'll be breathing deeply in sync with you. That's how you can make her "catch" *your* breath.

If she's dressed, tease her with her clothes. Remove them slowly, partially. Pull her blouse off her shoulder and caress that shoulder be-fore you take the blouse all the way off. Run your fingers under the inside edges of her bra before removing it. Play with her panties. Pull them between her vulva lips and up the crack of her ass. Don't take them off until the crotch is soaking wet.

A Word About Breast Touch

Please don't grab her titties! And don't grind them into her chest. Since female breasts are such sensitive structures, there's a fine line between stimulation and irritation, as every woman knows and every man who truly loves women ought to learn as soon as possible. Ac-cording to the Kinsey Institute, "about 90% of women receive some manual or oral breast stimulation" from their partners during sex. "But only about 50% of women say they actually enjoy breast stimu-lation, with many more saying they do it just because it gives plea-sure to their partners."[3] Some ladies say they always feel pain or discomfort when their breasts are touched, while others find it un-comfortable only right before menstruation.

[3]June M. Reinisch, *The Kinsey Institute New Report on Sexuality* (New York: St. Martin's Press, 1990), p. 104.

One reason so many ladies don't enjoy breast stimulation is a lack of communication. Their partners are doing what they *think* arouses women, when, in fact, it doesn't. Some communication about touch can be nonverbal, of course, but if that doesn't work, ask her what she likes, how lightly or firmly to touch, and where. Most women like soft squeezing and caressing around the whole breast, licking, sucking, and gentle biting around the nipple. Many like to have their breasts held up from underneath. *Some* even enjoy having their breasts grabbed, but *only* when highly aroused! The good news is, if you treat them right, a lady's nipples are powerful pleasure points with a *hot line* to her clitoris. Some lucky ladies, 1 percent according to Kinsey, can even have orgasms from nipple stimulation alone.[4]

Wet Touch

Pure and simple H_2O is one of *the* great, life-endowing aphrodisiacs—sipping it, soaking in it, swimming in it, surfing it, spraying it all over your body, letting it run between your legs, squirting water pistols, throwing water balloons (well, those are great aphrodisiacs if you're ten), utterly immersing yourself and your primemate into pools, showers, candlelit bubblebaths, crystal lakes, ocean waves, waterfalls, hot tubs, ice dips, thundershowers, golden showers, and long lovely walks in the rain. Our ancestors came from the sea, and as fetuses, we're nurtured in a warm, watery womb. Being immersed in or showered by water relaxes your resistance, engulfs you, makes you feel kind of like you're in the womb again. Inside and out, water cleanses you, washing away layers of physical and mental debris, loosening you up for love and other good things in life. For ladies, wetness is essential to orgasm.

> *Just as in real estate, where it's "location, location, location,"*
> *when it comes to female sexual pleasure,*
> *it's lubrication, lubrication, lubrication.*

Draw her a bubblebath lit by candles. Lick and suck her from toes to nose (see Lady's Commandment #9: Thou Shalt Have Foreplay, page 59) Always make sure her clitoris is lubricated when you touch it so that the friction doesn't hurt or tickle her.

[4]Ibid.

Pleasure and Pain

Pain is strange, isn't it? It can be really *bad*, especially when you aren't asking for it and it threatens your life. But when you do ask for it, when you voluntarily surrender to certain kinds of pain—like being squeezed, spanked, or penetrated hard by someone you love and trust—pain *can* be a healing, pleasurable release of tension and toxins. People into consensual sadomasochism (SM) often enjoy the pleasure of pain under controlled circumstances (see Lady's Commandment #10: Thou Shalt Find Out What Her Dreams Are Made Of, pages 71–84). This could be for any number of reasons too complex for the scope of this book, but one reason the lady in your life might be "into pain" is that she grew up with it. Maybe she was very sick or injured as a child, or perhaps she was spanked a lot. Then she grew up associating certain kinds of pain with attention and love and pleasure. Actually, the trauma of birth itself causes almost all of us to associate love and attention with pain.

Now, if you don't think you're "into pain," think again. Do you enjoy deep, pressure point massage? That's pretty painful; if it's effective, it is. Why do you think you actually like that kind of pain, and maybe other kinds, too, like the athletic ache of exercise or the light sting of a love spank or maybe a little lovebite? I'll tell you why. Because there's nothing like a little voluntarily inflicted pain to make you feel really alive. It's releasing, it's healing, it's stimulating, it's arousing, it's pleasure, it's pain. Appreciate it. Enjoy it. Take advantage of those precious, painful pressure points nature gave you all over your body and hers. But be careful now—everything in moderation—don't really hurt yourself, and, whatever you do, don't ever really hurt anybody else. Doctor's orders.

Toegasms
One of the nicest, most healing and sexy things you can do for the lady in your life is to massage her feet. After carrying all that weight around all day, often while tightly swaddled in oddly shaped shoes, her feet ache for the tender pressure of loving fingers. Reflexology and shiatsu are systems of foot massage based upon the tiny electrical reflexes in the bottoms of your feet that correspond to every part of your body. When you massage these pressure points in the feet, you stimulate the corresponding body part with healing energy. It's a

great, deliciously cleansing tension releaser. Pressure points can be pleasure points. After the massage, gently stroke her feet, running your fingers between her toes, caressing her ankles. Then maybe a little tickling, licking, and toe sucking. Sometimes, when Max sucks or rubs my big toe, I feel like it's a sexual organ, and I practically have an orgasm! I call it a toegasm.

A helpful hint for foot fanciers: If you want to suck your lover's foot and she's just too ticklish to take it, try massaging the foot first, which tends to relax it so it won't go into shock when it goes in your mouth. For a very sensual foot massage, use a little oil or lotion. Every foot lover has a favorite lubricant. Mary Magdalene used myrrh on Jesus' feet. You can use olive oil, vitamin E oil, perfumed lotion for sniffing, and flavored oil for sucking. Castor oil isn't too sexy, but it does get rid of calluses.

Foot massage is a great safe-sex activity; it's healthful, sexy, and doesn't require any exchange of body fluids. It's also a nice way to get very *sensual* without getting too directly sexual on a date, a good "first move" to make. Not many ladies turn down a foot massage, unless you've already turned her off by smelling like that overheated buffalo! Playwright Arthur Miller is said to have won the heart of Marilyn Monroe the night they met when he rubbed her big toe and looked deep into her love-hungry eyes.[5]

Eargasms

Try massaging her ears. Take out all her earrings, and really rub her ears hard. The ears are mostly cartilage, so they can take it. Insert your fingers right into her ears (make sure your fingernails are trimmed and clean); really finger those ears! Now lick and suck and tongue the sensitive depths of her inner ears.

Let her hear the ocean in the wetness of your tongue.

Rub her vulva at the same time with a free hand or give her a vibrator to use on herself, and you'll give her an exquisite *eargasm*.

Kinky Touch

So-called kinky touch might include spanking, tickling, vibrators, roughhousing (see aforementioned "Pleasure and Pain"). Make sure

[5]Irving Wallace, *The Intimate Sex Lives of Famous People* (London: Arrow Books, 1981), p. 313.

this is really what *she* wants; not just what you get off on. Don't make fun of her for wanting it. Talk to her about *how* she might like kinky touch. Experiment. Be careful not to hurt each other. Be a gentle-man, even when you roughhouse.

You might want to include a little bondage in your touch adventures. Tie her up, spank her buns, caress her all over, tickle her with a feather, rub ice or drip hot wax on her skin. She might really enjoy the body rush she gets by straining against the bonds, or the psychological excitement she feels by being "helpless." Then, again, she may panic from the loss of control. Respect her limits, and encourage her to voice them. No gags, please, and no neck ties besides simple collars, when either one of you is new to bondage.

Keep in mind that the way she does or doesn't like to touch and be touched has a lot to do with how her parents touched her. Find out as much as you can about her upbringing to better touch her heart through the surface of her skin (see Lady's Commandment #5: Thou Shalt Listen to Her, page 39).

Worshipful Touch
Help her to get in touch with her "Goddess Nature," her ability to feel worthy of being worshipped, by worshipping her body with your hands or tongue. Basically, you can use any of the "touch techniques" described above, but do so with a devout, adoring attitude. In worshipping her body with reverence, you honor her soul. We *are* our bodies, after all. Neither our minds, spirits, or souls are separate. They are part of our bodies—at least, for the time being.

Sensory Deprivation
Sensory deprivation turns sensory stimulation on its head. This can be very exciting, enhancing the senses that are not being deprived, e.g., depriving her sense of sight with a blindfold enhances her sense of smell and hearing. You might deprive her of movement by tying her up or holding her down (with her consent, of course). Notice how deprivation heightens her sensations, especially to being touched.

You Be the Touchee
Give pleasure to her fingertips by letting her touch you wherever she wants. Too often for most females' tastes, the human male tends

to be very cock-centered. Impatient when a lady slowly explores his arms, legs, chest, and face with her fingertips, he pushes her hands down to his penis—as if she didn't know where it was! Relax, take deep, eroticizing breaths, and let her touch you all over, even in "embarrassing" places. Let her tie you up, if you can handle the helplessness. You may surprise yourself, and find that you can have eargasms, too!

Sensitize Your Fingertips to Touch

If you or she has "trouble" with touch, or if you just want to explore a different way of touching, try an exercise that sex surrogates use to help touch-phobic clients get in touch with themselves. It's called *sensate focus*. There are many whole books written about sensate focus, but basically, it involves focusing on the simple act of touching, taking turns touching each other's bodies, concentrating on the sensations in your fingertips as you touch, or in whichever of your body parts that's being touched. Do sensate focus touching for several weeks without sexual intercourse, and you'll discover a whole new world of sensation that's literally at your fingertips!

Touch Is a Full-Time Job

To give a lady pleasure through touch, be tactile *all the time*, not just when you want sex. If you only touch her when you want sex, she will feel used and taken for granted. Hold hands, hug, stroke her skin for the sheer calming pleasure of touch. As the anthropologist Ashley Montagu pointed out, it is from loving touch that we obtain not only extreme pleasure but also comfort when we are in pain, relaxation when we're tense, and that simple yet miraculous certainty that we are not alone in this uncertain world.[6]

Recommended Reading
Ackerman, Diane. *A Natural History of the Senses.* New York: Random House, 1990.

[6]Ashley Montagu, *Touching: The Human Significance of the Skin* (New York: Harper & Row, 1986).

Kaplan, Helen Singer. *The Illustrated Manual of Sex Therapy*. New York: Brunner/Mazel, 1987.

Keesling, Barbara. *Sexual Pleasure: Reaching New Heights of Sexual Arousal & Intimacy*. Alameda, CA: Hunter House, 1993.

Kennedy, Adele P., and Susan Dean. *Touching for Pleasure*. Chatsworth, CA: Chatsworth Press, 1988.

3

Thou Shalt

Compliment Her Meaningfully

and Often

Just because you've told her once doesn't mean you shouldn't tell her again and again and again. Vary the type of compliment, and make it sincere, but keep pouring on the praise, and you will pleasure the "typical" female.

Compliment Connoisseurs

Ladies are exhibitionists. Not all ladies, of course. Just most ladies. Or, at least, a part of most ladies. The female generally likes to show off in some way, and be applauded and appreciated for who she is and what she does. For various psychosocial reasons, most women are also very insecure about all this, which is why they both crave compliments and don't know quite how to respond to them. But no matter how much a lady demurely blushes and protests, rest assured that she is a connoisseur of compliments. So is a gentleman; this commandment definitely goes both ways.

Experience helps. When a woman is frequently complimented, she can learn to really enjoy it and be gracious about it.

Praise the Lady

There is an art to being an appreciative voyeur and "giving good compliment" without sounding like a sniveling sycophant. When a woman looks down her nose at a guy who compliments her, it's because (a) he turns her off for other reasons, e.g., he has food on his face or smells like Napoleon before his bidet, or (b) he's giving her the wrong kind of compliment. Basically, the type of compliment you should give depends on the woman, but here's a flexible rule of thumb:

> *If she thinks she's plain, tell her she's beautiful.*
> *If she thinks she's beautiful, tell her she's smart.*
> *If she thinks she's smart, better tell her she's both!*

And don't just leave it at that. Tell her exactly *what* is so beautiful. But please, don't tell a strange woman she's got "great tits" or a "nice ass." Be a gentleman.

Give Her Attention

Be her biggest fan. Tell her she's a goddess. Don't worry about doing it with a straight face; *just do it.* Worship her body, and she'll be more likely to want to share it with you. Respect her mind, and she will give you the key to unlock her desires.

Compliment her on whatever she does well—her work, the way she keeps her home, the way she raises her kids, the way she treats her friends. Be a cheerleader on her team.

Raise Her Self-Esteem: You Can Do It

The average modern female is deeply insecure about her looks. Often, she is literally crippled with anxiety, shy, frightened, obsessed with her weight, her pimples, wrinkles, "unsightly" cellulite, or "unmanageable" hair, unable even to try to do the things she wants to do in life for fear that her looks just don't cut it.

As most of the mainstream media is so focused on women with perfect, airbrushed, implanted, virtually bionic bodies, piled on top of society's generally negative attitude toward female sexuality, it's no wonder that almost every woman alive struggles with the undertow of "low self-esteem."

So-called experts will tell you that the only people who can raise a woman's self-esteem are herself and her therapist. That's simple psychobabble. You, yes, *you* can help raise a woman's self-esteem just by complimenting her. The key is to do it *sincerely* (if, upon deep reflection, you can't sincerely sing her praises in any way, what are you doing with this woman?), *creatively* (make your compliments amusing, humorous, provocative, meaningful, inspirational), and *relentlessly* (no matter how well you know her, no matter how many times you've complimented her, *you must not cease the flow of praise!*). If you do compliment her sincerely, creatively, and relentlessly, you will make her feel better about herself (which often translates to feeling better about you, her biggest fan), and neither of you will run up a therapy bill.

> *By regularly showering her with artful, yet honest and meaningful compliments, and using selective inattention to her negative qualities, you can actually raise her self-esteem, no matter how low it is.*

Contrary to what many people believe, although the basis of a woman's self-esteem is laid down in early childhood and adolescence, it can change dramatically later on. A woman who was physically or emotionally beaten as a kid *can* learn to love, trust, be happy, and enjoy sex with a lover who adores and respects her, who lets her know that through both his actions and his compliments.

At the same time, even ladies with generally high levels of self-esteem have periods of doubt and feelings of failure. The most gorgeous women worry about wrinkles, the most brilliant women worry about whether they're really "big fakes," and the most unselfish women worry that they're not doing enough to help others. Praise her beauty, intelligence, and goodness, and acknowledge her achievements—whether it's making a great ratatouille, winning a tough case, doing a good job with the kids, or putting together a hot outfit. Let her know you're really proud of her, and her self-esteem will rise like home-baked bread. And you didn't know you could cook, did you?

> *Feeling beautiful, smart, and adored will make her feel very sexy.*

Josh, a caller to my radio show, told me he didn't understand why his wife Geena never put on the skimpy lingerie he adored. Turned out that Geena was slightly overweight, and though Josh really liked her voluptuousness, he hadn't told her so in years. I told him to sing her praises, send her cards, and hurry to make up for lost time! Three weeks later, he called back with the good news: Shortly after he started sincerely, creatively, and relentlessly praising her body, she began adorning it with the sexy silk teddies and g-strings he loved.

Criticism Is a Turn-Off

One of the biggest complaints about men that I hear from my female clients is: "He constantly criticizes me." And their husbands wonder why they're not interested in sex! What woman wants to make lovey-dovey to a man who's just told her that she's "turning into a baby elephant" or said that she "doesn't know what she's talking about" in front of a party of friends?

This doesn't mean that you should never offer constructive criticism. Just try to wrap criticisms up in compliments, as in, "Your hair has such a wonderful texture; it would look great cut a little shorter." Please don't say things to hurt her, even if you think they're "for her own good."

Compliment Her During Sex
Tell her how lovely she is, that her scent is delicious, that you adore the shape of her breasts, that her feet are precious, her lips luscious, her vulva an exquisite jungle of delights (in your own words, please).

> *Let your compliments touch her heart*
> *as your fingertips touch her skin.*

Simply saying her name (or pet name) often, especially during sex, is a great way to compliment her subtly. Her name is a powerful sound; no other word quite so arouses her. Say it as if you were saying it for the first time. Whisper it into her ear as she comes . . .

Compliment Her Taste
Compliment her whenever she gets dressed up, wears something different, or in any way seems to have put some effort into how she looks. Ladies become frustrated when men don't notice. A beautiful woman loves to be complimented on her clothes (especially her shoes!), because though her beauty may be God-given, her taste in clothes is a sign of her intelligence. Complimenting her clothes is a

great way to approach a lady you don't know at a party or other event. Needless to say, complimenting her clothes does not mean saying, "I like that low-cut top you're wearing," or, "Hey now, babe, that's a really short skirt." And don't be stupid, e.g., don't say, "I love the way your shoes match your eyes," unless they really do.

Put It in Writing

Commit your compliments to paper. Send them to her or, if you live together, leave them lying in wait for her. The medieval troubadours did this. One of the great courtly love traditions was writing love letters, ardently composed declarations of praise and passion to inflame the heart of a lady (see Lady's Commandment #7: Thou Shalt Give Her Things, pages 49–51).

Find special ways to sing her praises. Paint her, photograph her, videotape her. Publish her poetry, put it on the Internet, with her permission, of course. Compose a song about her. Show her off from every angle of her life. Get others to compliment her. Don't worry, it won't "spoil" her. It will only give her pleasure.

Recommended Reading
Rostand, Edmund. *Cyrano de Bergerac*, trans. Lowell Blair. New York: Signet Classics, 1972.
Woodman, Marion. *Addiction to Perfection*. Toronto: Inner City Books, 1982.

4

THOU SHALT

Encourage Her to Show and Tell You

How She Likes to Be Touched

The Orgasmic Island of Mangaia

According to ethnographer D. C. Marshall, the most orgasmically advanced people are on the Polynesian island of Mangaia.[1] Almost all Mangaian females have two or three orgasms each time they have sex. Why? you may ask, drool running down your mouth. Upon entering puberty, Mangaian boys go through a series of initiation rites instructing them in methods of stimulating women to maximize sexual pleasure. A Mangaian woman is *expected* to reach orgasm during intercourse each time; if not, the Mangaian man who fails to please her loses face. Two weeks after initiation, an experienced older woman begins training boys of around thirteen or fourteen in the art of giving pleasure to women. According to Marshall, Mangaians know more about female sexuality than most Western doctors. The Mangaians do not consider female sexual pleasure to be an extra. They believe it is absolutely necessary to a successful, fulfilling sexual union. High societal expectations of female orgasm have led to a high frequency of female orgasm. This is important because female

---

[1] Quoted in Lynn Margulis and Dorion Sagan, *Mystery Dance: On the Evolution of Human Sexuality* (New York: Simon & Schuster, 1990), p. 62.

pleasure, far more than male pleasure, is based upon societal expectations and sex education.

Can you imagine if our society formally instructed young men in how to please women?

Make Like the Mangaians

Since we don't have Mangaian initiation rites that teach the art of pleasing a lady through hands-on (not to mention tongues-on) demonstrations, you must create your own. Encourage your lady to be your Mangaian initiatrix, to show and tell you what gives her pleasure—before sex, during sex, after sex—whenever you can get her to open up and spill the goodies.

Many men are ambivalent about learning exactly how to give a woman pleasure. They say they want to learn, but when confronted by a lady's actual suggestions or requests, they often balk, feeling that they are being corrected or criticized. Whether you're the type that can't bear to ask for directions when you're lost on the road is your business. But if you can't handle a little *friendly* sexual direction from your female primemate, you're going to flunk the pleasure-giving test every time.

Jumping the Hurdles of Her Hang-Ups

If you can handle it, good for you! But you're not yet home free. Even if *you're* not intimidated by the frank expression of her desires, her past lovers may well have been, and she may be afraid you will be, too. The modern female is often confronted with the modern male's mixed messages of being desired for her *sexiness* but not for her sexual *assertiveness*. You may well have to reassure her and reiterate that it's okay for her to tell you what turns her on.

Another problem revolves around our modern idea of "soulmates." Secretly, a woman may feel that if you're her soulmate, and if you really love her, you'll know exactly what to do to bring her to the heights of erotic pleasure. But even soulmates need a little sex education when it comes to seriously pleasing each other. Though you don't necessarily have to enroll in some sort of college of carnal knowledge; for the most part, you can educate each other.

Some women might believe that sex shouldn't be talked about. Such people tend to dress privately and always have sex in the dark, never ever discussing it. They may excuse this behavior by saying that it "keeps the mystery going," but it's usually just an effort to mask inhibition, insecurities, and other unresolved sexual issues. One way to overcome this lack of communication is to read sex books, look at erotic art, or watch sex videos together, and then discuss them. There are many ways to "break the ice" and get a sexual conversation going. If you can afford it, hire an erotic dance troupe to come to your castle, and review it . . . together.

Your lady may set up other roadblocks to your discovery of her pleasure—the inhibitory possibilities are endless! Don't forget you're up against thousands of years of female sexual repression here. You may have to coax and convince her to tell you what she likes. So: Thou shalt coax and convince! Down on your knees and beg, if you must. It's worth it!

And don't just ask her what she likes once, then assume you know all about her tactile needs. Her pleasure points change; try to keep abreast (so to speak) of these changes. For more on how to tune into her tactile and other sensory needs, see Lady's Commandment #2: Thou Shalt Stimulate Her Senses (page 11).

Masturbation Mythology and Reality

Sometimes an image is worth a thousand instructions. So, request that your lady masturbate in front of you. Some ladies do this naturally; others are even more reluctant to *show* you what turns them on than they are to talk about it. After all, "playing with yourself," as harmless, healthful, and healing as we now know it to be, is still considered a forbidden act by many in our society.

Our modern social taboo against masturbation probably began as a practical code to sustain agrarian culture and tribal wars. Way back in Old Testament times, when Onan was ostracized for "spilling his seed upon the ground"[2] (actually, more of a case of *coitus interruptus* than masturbation), it was thought that if folks were masturbating

---

[2]For Onan's story, see Genesis 38:9 in your Bible.

instead of reproducing, they wouldn't spawn enough children to work their harvests or go to war against opposing tribes. Talk about membership drives—this was a big one.

Medieval Christians went on to further denigrate masturbation by equating sexual pleasure with pure evil. Since they didn't see any purpose to masturbation other than pleasure,[3] they declared it to be a major sin, one of the worst acts a person could commit. Over the centuries, frightening superstitions built up, e.g., that jacking or jilling off caused warts, blindness, insanity, hair on the palms, impotence, not to mention, of course, eternal damnation in hell (hmm, wonder if one can masturbate in hell, that might actually make it bearable—*beat your meat in the heat!*).

Modern science has proven all these superstitions about masturbation to be 100 percent wrong.

Even though an American Surgeon General[4] was fired just for mentioning it in the context of safe-sex education, experts consider masturbation to be a healthy, normal, very safe sexual activity.

There's even some positive folklore on the wonders of whacking off. According to the Greeks, masturbation was a divine gift. Hermes revealed the technique to Pan, whose love for a nymph went unfulfilled, and Pan then taught the shepherds (maybe so they wouldn't bother their poor sheep so much!). The Greek philosopher Diogenes praised the extraordinary physical efficiency of masturbation: "Would to heaven that it were enough to rub one's stomach in order to allay one's hunger."

In any case, as comedian George Carlin said, "If God had intended us not to masturbate, he would have made our arms shorter."

Despite masturbation's radical "rehabilitation" in the eyes of scientists and sex experts, it remains taboo with many people. Now, instead of fearing masturbation will make them blind, many worry that it will brand them as lonely and desperate or "oversexed." Masturbating with a partner present obviously has nothing to do with loneliness, but novices may feel uncomfortably vulnerable about it anyway.

---

[3]Though now we know that wanking isn't *just* fun, it's good for maintaining sexual health, especially when you don't have a partner.
[4]Dr. Joycelyn Elders.

Out of fear and ignorance, some women never even masturbate by themselves, let alone in front of anyone. Often, such women don't even *know* how they like to be touched. Be sensitive to your lady's fears and inhibitions. Don't try to force her to do anything she doesn't want to do, but don't give up your coaxing. Reassure her of your love and respect for her. Get her a copy of *Sex for One* by Dr. Betty Dodson, the pioneer "mother of masturbation," or take her to an Annie Sprinkle performance. You may be able to get her into the spirit by "going first" and masturbating in front of her.

Learn to Drive Her Vulva

Once you've got her "petting the kitty," watch her carefully, *very* carefully, not just for your own excitement—though it *is*, of course, very exciting—but to *see* how she likes to be touched.

Get a good look at her vulva. It's not a Swedish automobile, darling, but you still should learn to "drive" it, not to mention give it a "tune-up." Object of lust, source of life, center of pleasure, mouth of Mother Nature, Beauty to some, Beast to others, the vulva can be a mystery to both men and women.

Physically speaking, the vulva consists of outer labia or *labia majora*, the "doors to the temple," the fleshy hairy lips you can see; the inner labia or *labia minora*, those succulent inside lips that swell with excitement; and the clitoris, Little Red Riding Hood, her pleasure center, the Jewel in the Lotus, the precious pearl of her luscious oyster. Mmmm . . . sounds tasty . . . It is.

The vulva is the most beautiful part of the female body to some;
a sexual terror to others.

The playwright Tennessee Williams is said to have told actress Elizabeth Ashley that when he was taken to a brothel for his "initiation into manhood," a prostitute made him look between her legs. "All I could see was something that looked like a dying orchid," he said. "Consequently, I have never been comfortable either with orchids or women." Now, Tennessee turned out to be almost 100 percent gay, but a lot of heterosexual men aren't very comfortable with the appearance of the female vulva. But listen, guys, the more comfortable you get, the better lover you'll be. Of course, if you've got a very talented tongue, you can always make like a mole and do it in the dark.

Some unfortunate gentlemen genuinely fear the vulva and vagina. The myth of the vagina with teeth (*vagina dentata*) exists in many cultures. Metaphorically, every vagina has secret teeth, for the male exits as less than when he entered. But listen, you yokels, no vagina has real teeth (though a misplaced IUD may feel like a fang)!

So, go on, take a good long look. Watch how her inner labia swell, redden, and moisten as she gets more and more aroused. See how her clitoris starts to jut out as it gets juiced up. Look at how she pulls and plays with her vulva lips, and fingers her clit. Does she touch it directly, circle around it, play above, below, over to the left, or the right? Notice if she squeezes her butt, fingers her anus, pinches her nipples, twirls her pubic hair, spanks herself. Pay particular attention to the way she touches herself right before she comes. Don't get so lost in watching that you forget to tell her how beautiful she looks.

Get Wild
Once she realizes you like watching her, you can tease more and more of the exhibitionist out of her. Encouragement and acceptance invite that inner showoff to come out and dance. Watch out, she may get wild! For variety, give her a vibrator, a bottle of almond oil, a dildo (if you don't have a regular one, use a cucumber, carrot, or banana—nature's own dildos), a couple of ben wa balls maybe, and watch your lady wail . . .

Someone to Watch Over Me
By encouraging your female primemate to show you how she likes to be touched, not only will you learn how to touch her to give her pleasure, you'll be giving her pleasure just by "letting" her masturbate in front of you. Even if she's not much of an exhibitionist, masturbation is fun, easy, direct, intimate, and ought to be a part of anybody's sexual repertoire, with and without a partner. It's a brilliant light into the window of life, keeping us in loving touch with our physical selves no matter what our relationship status. When my female clients tell me that they find it difficult to orgasm with intercourse, I usually suggest that they masturbate *during* intercourse (there's al-

ways a way for her to slide a wet finger or two over to her clit), and that almost always brings about a wonderful, penis-gripping climax.

In an odd way, watching "over her" as she masturbates can make her feel safe, cared for, accepted in her most vulnerable state, even protected and "looked" after.

If you follow this commandment,
you will become what every female wants:
"Someone to watch over me."

Recommended Reading

Barbach, Lonnie, and Linda Levine. *Shared Intimacies*. New York: Double-day, 1980.

Blank, Joani, ed. *Femalia*. San Francisco: Down There Press, 1993.

Dodson, Betty. *Sex for One*. New York: Harmony Books, 1987.

Walker, Alice. *Possessing the Secret of Joy*. New York: Harcourt Brace Jo-vanovich, 1992.

5

THOU SHALT

Listen to Her . . .

. . . and learn about who she is, what she's been through, what she needs, and what she wants. The most frequent complaint that women have about men is that they don't listen.

Why couldn't Freud figure out "what women wanted"? Because Freud didn't want to hear. Freud didn't want to listen. And listening was his profession! But he was too busy formulating theories to bother really listening to the ladies in his life. Not that Freud was unusual. Most Victorian men discounted the conversation of women as being not far above the prattle of toddlers. Perhaps that's one reason (besides punishingly tight corsets) that Victorian ladies were always fainting. Since men didn't listen to them, at least passing out got their attention!

Ladies Need to Talk

The modern woman gets a bit more respect and attention to what she has to say. But she *needs* a lot more. Overworked and underpaid at home and on the job, the contemporary female has a tremendous need to talk about her feelings and *to be heard*, just to cope with her humongous stress. And, since she's busier than ever, she has more to talk about than ever before.

So, even if you're hyperactive and hard of hearing, listen up!

In following this commandment, you have three main goals: Listen to please, listen to support, and listen to learn.

Listen to Please

For the female, talking is foreplay. She doesn't have to talk about sex. She could talk about work, gossip, or what the kids did to drive her crazy that day. Whether gushing rhapsodically or complaining cathartically, just talking is a release for her. It actually helps her to breathe easier. And, as we learned under Lady's Commandment #2: Thou Shalt Stimulate Her Senses (page 11), breathing easily is very important for good sex.

Most gentlemen have a hard time comprehending how talking about something that has nothing to do with sex can put a lady in a sexual mood, but it can and it does. Before the female can appreciate romance, she often needs to talk and to be heard, to feel understood for who she is and what she's going through.

The need for sympathy and someone to talk to is a major cause of female infidelity, much bigger than dissatisfaction with her main male's thrusting techniques.

Karen called my radio show because she felt guilty about having a secret love affair. At first, she couldn't even say just why she was involved with her lover, who was less successful, less good-looking, and even less exciting than her husband; she just knew she felt relaxed and sexual with him in a way she never felt with her husband. When I asked her what she thought she could do with her lover that she couldn't do with her husband, she laughed and replied, "I can talk."

And apparently, her lover listens. He asks questions. He seems to be genuinely interested. She talks about her life, her opinions, her feelings, her fears, her fantasies. And he listens. Karen's husband never listens. He's too busy working, playing tennis, watching TV, or talking himself. Oh, she talks to her husband about basic stuff, like household chores and the evening news, but rarely about her feelings, never about her fantasies. And she needed someone to talk to. She started talking to her lover at the office where they both worked; that led to talking over lunch, then talking over dinner, then talking over drinks at his place, then talking in bed. She couldn't believe how she'd talked herself into a full-blown secret love affair. If only her husband had listened. . . .

> *The female needs to have someone to talk to. If she can't talk to you, she'll talk to someone else, and that might just make her horny for whomever is listening.*

And she doesn't just need for you to listen to her for a few minutes before nookie-time. If you want a decent love life, your primemate needs to feel heard and understood on an ongoing basis.

In the beginning of a relationship, she doesn't need it *so* much. After all, she doesn't know you very well, and she can pretend that you understand her. But as time goes on, and she realizes that you don't actually have an amazing psychic awareness of her innermost thoughts and feelings, her need for you to listen to her becomes essential to her loving you, both mentally and physically. At that point, if you aren't listening, you won't be getting laid.

Talking about sex will also make her feel better about sex, especially when it comes to trying anything new. Most ladies have been raised on the notion that sex is dirty, forbidden stuff that mustn't be talked about. The more she talks about her feelings of sexual guilt and shame, sorting out where they come from and what they really mean, the less guilty and shameful she is likely to feel and the more open she will be to erotic pleasure.

Listen to Support

There's a reason that so many ladies fall in love with their therapists. It's not because they're so smart. It's certainly not because they're good-looking. It's because they *listen to support.*

Support means listening to her hopes and dreams, her fears and insecurities with real understanding, not just a perfunctory "uh-huh." Support means letting her cry or even yell and scream, offering comfort but not necessarily advice, unless she requests it. Support means letting her know that it is safe for her to share her real feelings. Support means not rushing to judge or "rescue" her or solve her "problems," unless she asks for your help. Support means listening without anger, anxiety, or disapproval. That's not easy, but if you get mad at her when she tells you what she feels, she won't feel safe sharing her feelings with you. That may well translate into "no nookie" because if she can't share her feelings, why would she want to share her body with you?

Support means listening with empathy and compassion. In our masculinist society, most little boys are raised to denigrate emotions like empathy and compassion as too feminine, soft, and weak. These emotions may well be feminine and even soft, but they are by no means weak; they form the bedrock of happy, trusting, pleasurable relationships.

> *We will all be better off when both men and women take pride*
> *in feeling and expressing their softer, tender, sympathetic sides.*

You Will Be Tested

If you've tried to listen to her, but you really just wish she'd shut up most of the time, you probably shouldn't be with her. If for some reason, you can't or don't want to leave her (e.g., she's the mother of your children, is totally devoted to you, makes killer lasagna, and gives great head), force yourself to listen as if she were your teacher and you will be tested on everything she says.

Listen to Learn

Listening to her not only gives her pleasure and support, it gives you information. Listen to learn about her sexual desires. Encourage her to talk not only about how she likes to be touched, but how she feels about sex in general or a particular sexual activity that you're interested in exploring. Listen to her fears and hesitations as well as her passions and fantasies. This is especially important if you've been trying to "get" her to do something she's reluctant to do. Maybe the reason she's so disinclined to oblige your fantasy is because you never listen to any of hers!

Listen and learn about her childhood, her relationships with her mother, father, brothers, sisters, how she was punished and rewarded.

Our sexual nature is formed when we are very young, so our family has a big impact on it, incest taboos notwithstanding.[1] If you listen carefully, you can glean some understanding of her sexual nature from the childhood stories she tells you. Was she a wallflower as a teen? That might explain why exhibitionism excites her so much. Was her family extremely religious and conservative? That could account for her uptightness about sex; then again, that might make her want to rebel, break taboos, and experiment sexually. Was she sick a lot, in and out of the hospital, or beaten as a child? That might point to an interest in bondage and other forms of SM.

It can be fun and erotic to listen to her childhood stories, sexual and otherwise. As long as you're not unreasonably jealous, sharing stories about first kisses, first feels, or first blow-jobs can be a tremendous aphrodisiac. You may even want to role-play a particularly arousing memory (see Gentleman's Commandment #7: Thou Shalt Discover His Deepest Desires and Fantasies, pages 143–146).

But sometimes listening means hearing her stories of pain, abuse, being lied to, forced into sex, abandoned, or disappointed. Obviously, listen as sympathetically as you can. If therapy seems like a good idea because she can't get beyond her past, suggest it. But don't overdo it.

Don't make her childhood worse than it really was!

Don't exploit her honesty and trust for the sake of your own moral agenda. If, for instance, she tells you she had sex at an early age but doesn't feel she was molested and doesn't feel bad about it, don't suggest that she *ought* to feel bad or turn herself in to the nearest victims group.

Keep in mind that the compelling nature of sex and our society's repressed attitude toward it are an extremely volatile combination, causing many otherwise "normal" people to have traumatic sex-related experiences as children or adolescents.

[1]For a deeper understanding of childhood and adolescent sexuality, see Dr. Michael E. Perry, *Handbook of Sexology.* Vol. 7, *Childhood and Adolescent Sexology,* eds. John Money and H. Musaph (New York: Elsevier, 1990).

> *Thanks to society's ongoing War on Sex, we are all walking wounded. Talking, and knowing that someone is listening, helps to heal the wounds.*

If she's shy about talking about herself, encourage her. It's worth your while, if only to find out who she is. But it will also give her pleasure, acknowledging her life as meaningful and interesting. One way to get her to talk about her childhood is to tell her something about yours. Not your entire, unabridged life story, darling! After all, you're supposed to be listening to *her* now. A few select scenes will do.

As you listen, you will discover the little girl inside your woman. There's a lot of talk about all men being little boys inside, and that's true, of course, but all ladies are little girls inside, too. Find the little girl inside your woman; pleasure her, play with her, and she'll never grow old. Talk to her and, most of all, *listen* to her, and she'll never stop speaking to you.

Recommended Reading

Tannen, Deborah. *You Just Don't Understand.* New York: William Morrow, 1990.

Gray, John. *Men Are from Mars, Women Are from Venus.* New York: Harper-Collins, 1992.

6

THOU SHALT

Make Her Laugh

Laughter is a mental orgasm. Amuse your lady. Play court jester. Be a fool for love. Act like a bonobo chimpanzee. Give her a glorious case of the giggles. Make her want to wet her panties, especially if you're into golden showers. Give her the gift of laughter (we'll get to other gifts at Lady's Commandment #7: Thou Shalt Give Her Things, page 49). "If somebody makes me laugh, I'm his slave for life," swore entertainer Bette Midler. Women love men or other women who make them laugh.

For what is pleasure, after all?
A relaxing of the defenses and an awakening of the senses
including your sense of humor.

What's the Big Deal?

Humor is vital, in part, because life itself can be so dreadfully serious. Humor has many important uses: it can help ease tension and frustration, soothe bad feelings, defuse an argument, put little problems in their place, or bring up bizarre sexual fantasies.

Laughter Is the Soundtrack to Playing

That might sound frivolous, but it's through playing that most great achievements are accomplished. Inventions, works of art, and discoveries of all kinds often come into being through play. And play (if you're doing it right) is pleasurable.

Humor is a key aspect of charm, whether the sophisticated and debonair variety or the cute and cuddly sort. Humor is seductive.

> *If you can make her laugh, you can win her heart,*
> *and her genitals will soon follow.*

When you make her laugh, you dissolve her fears and concerns about you, especially when your humor is a little self-deprecating. When you make fun of yourself a bit, it makes you less scary, less of a weighty presence for her to ponder and fret about. Many a lousy cad has gotten his way with women with nothing but a disarming sense of humor. Don't be a cad, of course, but do loosen up your funny bone.

The Comedy of Sex

Sex can be extremely funny, especially in the context of our uptight, sex-negative society. As the feminist/art historian/pornographer Camille Paglia declared, "Sex is a comedy, not a tragedy."[1]

Unfortunately, owing to a combination of biology and psychology, the male can be so goal-oriented about sex, so worried about "performance," that he fears mixing sex with humor. But the female tends to adore it, enjoying a lighter, teasing approach to sex (see Lady's Commandment #2: Thou Shalt Stimulate Her Senses, page 11).

In sex, sometimes you have to play a few tricks, even on yourself. Tricks like confessing how nervous you are in a cute, funny way or even role playing sexy yet amusing characters can help you to lift the *pressure* and find the *pleasure*. But tricks are okay—tricks are for kids, and we're all kids inside, especially when it comes to playing.

And bed (or the bath or the backseat of the car) is a great place to play all the games you ever wanted to play, to fool around with fool-

---

[1]Camille Paglia, *Vamps and Tramps* (New York: Vintage Books, 1994).

ish abandon, with freedom from old, outside taboos. A certain amount of unpredictability and spontaneity is very exciting. That brings me to the presentation of kinky ideas:

> *Try to include a little humor if you're introducing something new into your sex life, something that you suspect is rather wild for her tastes, like cross-dressing, exhibitionism, or even dominance and submission.*

Humor eases tension, distracts her from worrying about how weird you might be. And if she just can't deal with it, you can always say, "I'm only kidding" (though you may not want to, if your kink is important to you).

Cock of the Walk

If you're a closet exhibitionist yearning to expose yourself, just present your fetish with humor. Do an amusing striptease for her, to turn her on and make her laugh simultaneously; now *that's* pleasure. Even if you're not a great-looking, hard-bodied, Chippendales specimen, you're probably cute in some way. Emphasize your *cuteness*; ladies love and often forgive real cuties.

Max "exposes himself" to me quite often and quite humorously. After I laugh at his adorable antics until my face hurts, I often wind up giving him head. For more on acting out exhibitionism, see Lady's Commandment #10: Thou Shalt Find Out What Her Dreams Are Made Of (pages 78–79).

Humor Compatibility

Laughter can be very meaningful. If you can make her cry (with joy, of course) and laugh at the same time, you're really doing well. Make her laugh to cheer her up, though not to minimize or make fun of her feelings, of course. Tactful, nonjudgmental, gentle humor or wicked, insightful, politically incorrect wit, or just plain sidesplitting silliness—whatever turns her on!

Humor is quite subjective, of course. Humor compatibility is as important as a sexual "fit." Your friends and family may think you're hilarious, you may even have your own late-night TV talk show, but *she* may think you're a bore or maybe just an idiot, and then you're out of luck. If she doesn't like your humor, she probably doesn't really like you, even if you give her multiple orgasms and fabulous jewelry. That is, if her sense of humor leads toward amusing, satirical repartee, and your sense of humor involves dressing up in madras shorts and a propeller-topped beanie, you have a definite problem.

There are also different kinds of sexual humor. One woman's idea of sexual humor might be creative role playing, another's might be Naked Twister, though I suppose it's possible to combine the two: Just pretend you're Mata Hari and a hapless, sex-starved general playing Naked Twister as the bombs of the Great War drop outside your hotel room, throwing you into each other's arms and between each other's legs!

Everyone has a sense of humor. You just have to have the confidence to let yours out, to risk bombing just like the stand-up comics do.

No Insults, Please

Needless to say (though I do feel the need to say it), do NOT make jokes at her expense. Being insulted, even with supreme Noël Cowardesque wit, is not any woman's pleasure.

Recommended Reading

Heimel, Cynthia. *If You Leave Me, Can I Come Too?* New York: Atlantic Monthly Press, 1994.

———. *Get Your Tongue Out of My Mouth, I'm Kissing You Good-Bye!* New York: Atlantic Monthly Press, 1993 (and any of Heimel's sexy, feminist columns in *Playboy*; they'll give you a great understanding of what many ladies find witty and charming in men).

McGhee, Paul. *How to Develop Your Sense of Humor.* New York: Kendall-Hunt, 1994.

The comics pages of your local paper. My dad used to read them every day, and always made my mom—and everybody else—laugh.

7

THOU SHALT

Give Her Things

That's right: *Give* her things. Presents. Tokens. Gifts. Geegaws. Favors. Offerings. Ever since the dawn of humanity, when prehistoric men gave the best chunks of food to the women they desired (an essential mating arrangement that the British anthropologist Chris Knight calls "sex-for-meat"),[1] men have successfully seduced women with gifts.

The kind of gift depends on the lady and on you. It could be emerald earrings from Tiffany's, a flower you picked from a field (though please, not from her own front yard!), the gift of your emotional support or your creative talent. Sometimes the gift itself is an erotic pleasure—lingerie, a vibrator, a butt plug, a Greek island cruise. But any gift, even dinner and a movie, can be an aphrodisiac.

> *It's not that she doesn't love you for yourself; it's just that a very primitive part of her responds to a gift as an erotic act.*

What Good Are Gifts?

Gifts excite her. Gifts make her feel valued. Gifts stimulate her. Gifts make her feel safe, secure, provided for, cared for. The female needs

---

[1]Quoted in James Shreeve, *The Neandertal Enigma: Solving the Mystery of Modern Human Origins* (New York: William Morrow, 1995), p. 332.

to feel safe to relax and enjoy sex. When you don't give her anything but your body, she feels cheap, uncared for, certainly unprovided for.

Gifts are useful, and a lady tends to be, out of biological and social necessity, very *practical* about romance. Gifts have meaning to her. Gifts have power for her.

Gifts keep her company, reminding her of you when you're gone. Ever since Mommy gave her a pacifier, she's used "things" to temporarily substitute for the real "thing" that is the one she loves. This is the source of the legendary feminine lust for largesse.

> *Don't resent this aspect of so many women*
> *(translation: don't be cheap)! Make the most of it . . .*

What Should You Give Her?

Give gifts that are special for her, gifts that have meaning for her. Give her what will work for her, not just what works for you. If you have no idea what to get her, go with flowers. Find out which flowers she prefers. They won't remind her of you for more than a few days, but they're never wrong (unless she has allergies). If you can afford it and you've got similar tastes, jewelry and other wardrobe adornments, such as silk scarves or chic hats, are also good bets as pleasure gifts. So are items that help her with her work, like nice pens, fancy calculators, and date books (to make her think of you whenever she makes a date). If she likes to cook, get something for the kitchen— that's if *she* likes to cook, not just if *you* like to eat!

You can also create something special for her. Dedicate your next masterpiece to her. Paint her a picture. Write her a song. Or just call up the radio station she listens to and dedicate one to her.

These are just some general ideas. As you get to know her, learn her needs and wants, so you can get her the kind of gifts she'll squeal over with pleasure.

The Courtly Gift of Love Letters

One of the great courtly love traditions is sending love letters, passionate posts, hot notes, adoring epistles written in the ink of desire.

You know how spoken words—sweet nothings, orgasmic outcries, whispering fantasies—are all great aphrodisiacs. So are written words, words that endure, words committed to paper that one lover labored over so that the other could linger over each of them, lovingly. And they don't cost a thing but your time. Great love letters can be great literature—Shakespeare's sonnets, Anaïs Nin's letters to Henry Miller. But even love letters that won't win a Pulitzer can be tools of seduction. Love letters fuel the romantic imagination, stimulating an important human sex organ, the brain. If you've ever received a love letter from someone you love, you know how you cherish it, how your mind plays with every luscious word of it. If you've ever written a love letter, you know the thrill of creating poetry from passion, of rhapsodizing, spilling your soul onto creamy white sheets of paper.

In the times of the troubadours, every Lancelot would write thousands of pages to his Guinevere before even kissing her, and Cyrano de Bergerac could win a lady's heart with the power of his pen. With telephones, love letter writing almost became a lost art. Fortunately, the fax machine is reviving the art, *but* lovers, beware, you never know who might pick up your faxed fantasies on the other side of the machine. Better to send erotic E-mail through cyberspace.[2] Whether you send your love letters by mail, by fax, by cupid's bow or carrier pigeon, do write them and do send them. They are one of the most civilized aphrodisiacs on earth, excellent gifts for the literate lady.

Other Gift Ideas

Do Her Favors
Not only will you be giving her a gift, but you'll be reinforcing her dependence on you, not a bad thing if you're in love. Screw in a lightbulb, take out the trash, install a new program she wants into her computer, find her a lawyer or honest car mechanic, whatever she needs to have done. Doing little things for her is just like giving her little gifts. And they add up to making you a part of her life.

---

[2]Most computers let you password-protect files sent by E-mail, so no one but a dedicated hacker can read your love note without your password. Just make sure your primemate knows the magic word.

Lingerie Shopping Tips

It's debatable whether sexy lingerie is a gift for you or for her. If she can wear it anywhere besides to bed with you, you can consider it a gift for her.

Many of my male callers and clients ask me how to get the ladies in their lives to actually wear the lingerie they buy for them instead of just using it to line their drawers. So, here are my Two Most Important Lingerie Shopping Tips:

1. Just because something looks sexy to you doesn't mean it's going to make a lady feel sexy, especially if the person it looks sexy on is a model in a Victoria's Secret catalog as opposed to the woman you're giving it to. Gentlemen tend to be visual, but most ladies are more tactile, and from a lady's point of view, *feeling* sexy is what lingerie is all about. The softer the material, the better. Nothing rough like that cheap stuff you find in adult bookstores between the inflatable dolls and the eighteen-inch double-header dildos. When in doubt, get silk.

2. Know thy lady. Lingerie should not simply reveal her body parts; it should accentuate her individual beauty. Get to know what she looks good in. When in doubt about her size, get flowing, billowy lingerie, not tight stuff that might not fit her. If you want to see your lady in a tight push-up bra, take her shopping with you so she can get the fit and look that pleases you both.

   In some shops, you can even go into the dressing room with her. Max and I love to do that. It's a real exhibitionist-voyeur delight, spiced with the possibility of getting caught . . . especially when you start *testing* the lingerie with some serious fondling, and the saleslady cracks open the door and says, "Oops!" Great if you're into threesome fantasies.

Take Her Out

A great date, where you make the plans, get the tickets, pick the restaurant, drive the car, and take care of the details, is a kind of gift. Make sure you're taking her somewhere she likes to go. No fair going to see your favorite football team unless she's a genuine sports fan herself.

Take Her Shopping

If you don't know what to get her, take her shopping. This is not, of course, for the faint of heart. You must be patient, companionable, tolerant of having perfume samples spritzed into your face, and clever enough to steer her only to items you can afford. Don't go crazy and overload your munificence if you don't know her very well. Remember, diamonds are forever, but so are the payments, and your relationship with her may not be.

Recommended Reading

Catalogs from her favorite stores.
Sequoia, Anna. *The Official J.A.P. Handbook*. New York: Plume, 1982.

8

THOU SHALT

Exude Confidence and Vulnerability

Generally, for the female, confidence—even cockiness—is a strong aphrodisiac. Your confidence makes her feel secure and excited at the same time, assures her that you know what to do, that you can teach her a thing or two, and that you can be flexible if plans change.

Confidence is especially important for the male to turn on the female. In our society, shy ladies will often be approached, but shy gentlemen will usually be ignored (unless you're super-good-looking, you just won an Oscar, or your mom or dad own the company she works for).

What If You Don't Feel Confident?

If you don't *feel* confident, there's one thing you can do right off the bat, without a therapist, a support group, or even a self-help book: *Fake it*. While I don't advocate faking most other emotions—or orgasms—I think it's okay to fake confidence, because after you keep faking it for a while, you start to *feel* it.

Basically, "faking it," as I define it in this context, is a low-tech, self-guided form of *behavior modification*. You consciously replace discouraging thoughts with positive ones. You also replace negative, off-putting actions with affirmative, sociable ones. For instance, you force yourself to smile, even when you're nervous and feel more like grimacing, and at first you might feel strange or hypocritical; but eventually you find that you feel better and the people around you feel better, too.

You force yourself to act self-assured even when you're scared, and eventually you're as self-assured as an "assurance" salesman!

But don't *leave* it at faking it; otherwise, you'll become a superficial, uninformed, arrogant, bombastic jerk that no self-respecting female wants to hang around, unless you give her a *lot* of major gifts. Develop some real depth to your aura of confidence, and the aura will become actual.

Learn as much as you can about "the female," get in touch with your own feminine side, as well as your particular lady and her pleasure points. Your knowledge will give you a confidence in your ability to please her that can't be faked. Develop your confidence in *her*, too; if you can trust her, you'll feel more confident around her.

Surrender to Her

Feminist or traditional, most women do love a confident lover, unless they want to mother a lover, which most ladies do, *sometimes*. Hence the second part of this commandment: Thou shalt be vulnerable.

Let yourself be a little kid, *sometimes*. Surrender to her power. Be vulnerable to her. But don't fake vulnerability! That's tacky.

You can "make" yourself more vulnerable, though. You can talk more about your feelings. You can ask questions that expose your naïveté. You can admit your ignorance, when appropriate. You can force yourself to open up about things that scare you. If you won't do it for your own good (though it is good for you), do it for her. Remember:

Your vulnerability gives her a very satisfying, maternal, emotional, and even erotic kind of pleasure.

It makes you seem warmer and cuddlier. It makes you accessible, adorable, and lovable.

Combination Plate

If you can combine confidence with vulnerability, you're probably the kind of person who can talk about your feelings. Good for you! Most modern ladies love that.

> *The strong silent type is a sex symbol of the past, and a good thing, too, for he was often a secret psychopath.*

Too many boys in our society are taught contempt and disgust for soft "feminine" emotions like vulnerability. They are taught to be suspicious of sensitivity, which is associated with women and "sissies." Don't be a victim of the "masculine mystique" that says that "real men" can't be vulnerable.[1] There is absolutely no reason that gentlemen shouldn't be just as vulnerable and sensitive as ladies. In fact, most women are attracted to vulnerability and sensitivity in men (or other women), *as long as they're accompanied by confidence.*

What About Sex?

How can a man be sexually confident when he doesn't know what to do and needs to learn? Answer: First, be vulnerable. Have confidence in *your ability to learn* what you don't already know. Ironically, in our society, as opposed to the exotic, erotic isle of Mangaia, a man is supposed to know all about sexual pleasure without any sex education. He's certainly not supposed to ask his lady questions about what gives her pleasure and take time to discover the details of her desire.

Well, forget society, at least while you're in bed. *You* are supposed to ask questions, be vulnerable, and take time to discover her personal pleasures! *And that's a commandment!*

D&S Dynamics

The dynamic of confidence and vulnerability shows up in erotic dominance and submission (D&S) games. The dominant partner displays confidence, often dramatically, and the submissive partner is

[1]Myriam Miedzian, *Boys Will Be Boys: Breaking the Link Between Masculinity and Violence* (New York: Doubleday, 1991), p. xx.

vulnerable, usually to an extreme degree. Some of the erotic roles that fit this dynamic are Mistress and Slave, Master and Prisoner, Nurse and Patient, Teacher and Student, the Experienced One and the Virgin, Trainer and Trainee, and Boss and Employee. Some couples stick to one dynamic, but the healthiest couples tend to switch roles (see Gentleman's Commandment #7: Thou Shalt Discover His Deepest Desires and Fantasies, page 141).

A Gentle Manhood

The same dynamic also appears in the medieval troubadour ideal of "a more gentle manhood" (from which our term *gentleman* derives), a masculine ideal that was valiant and vulnerable, brave but not barbaric, chivalrous but not chauvinist, virile but not violent (relatively speaking).[2] One reason so many ladies went wild for the troubadours—while their brutal, graceless husbands and dads were off stabbing themselves and others in various horrific Crusades—was that the troubadours were courageous and sensitive, bursting with love, yet in control of their passions. This dynamic developed into modern courtship, a traditional point of female pleasure—when it's done well, that is.

Courtship requires courtesy.

The less confidence a lady has, the less power and the more vulnerability you should show her (unless you're role playing a dominance and submission fantasy). There's a fine but vital line between being a powerful male and being too overbearing. Don't be pushy, but don't be a pushover, either. Hey, I didn't say it was easy to find the right balance, just possible! And very worthwhile.

A Knight's Main Virtues

The courtship of a lady is an endless challenge, requiring the development of many talents and character traits.

---

[2] Riane Eisler, *Sacred Pleasure* (New York: HarperCollins, 1995), p. 32.

> *In the twelfth century, the Five Main Virtues of the Medieval*
> *Knight, the virtues that he cultivated to win the heart of his Lady,*
> *were: Temperance, Courage, Love, Loyalty, and Courtesy.*

Add being good at giving head, and I think you've got the Six Main Virtues of a Knight for the 1990s . . . which brings us to Lady's Commandment #9: Thou Shalt Have Foreplay. . . .

Recommended Reading
Cabot, Tracy. *Man Power.* New York: St. Martin's Press, 1988.
Harris, Thomas. *I'm OK—You're OK.* New York: Harper & Row, 1969.

9

THOU SHALT

Have Foreplay

oreplay: The word itself sounds trivial, like an insubstantial appetizer with intercourse as the main course. But for the female, all the holding, teasing, kissing, licking, spanking, lovebiting, caressing, cuddling, and other kinds of "outercourse" that we lump into this utterly unworthy term *foreplay* can be more pleasurable than actual genital intercourse.

When Does Foreplay Happen?

Foreplay doesn't all have to happen in bed, minutes before sex. It can happen over a hug and a squeeze in the middle of the day, a long luscious kiss over lunch, or a hand up her skirt and between her warm thighs during dinner.

Any kind of affectionate touch can be foreplay.

Holding your lady's hand at the movies is foreplay. Rubbing the back of her neck as she works at her desk is foreplay. Kissing her while she brushes her teeth with a mouthful of toothpaste is deliciously, sputteringly silly foreplay.

Max and I spend the majority of our day engaged in foreplay. Since we also tend to spend the majority of our day working, that means mixing business with pleasure pretty constantly. Much to the good-humored nausea of our employees, we are forever sneaking smooches and squeezes between meetings and phone calls. As devoted prime-mates, we believe in staying "in touch," literally, all day long.

Foreplay Is Playful

If you're tense about sex, do something to loosen yourself up. Get in touch with your inner child. Make like a bonobo chimpanzee. Take up yoga. Move to the music. Have a drink. Take a bubblebath. Do a little deep breathing. Whatever you do, *do whatever is necessary to get playful*. Stiff, tense, mechanical foreplay is no play, as far as most women are concerned.

Be sensitive to the rhythm at which she likes to be touched. Soft and gentle? Hot and rough? Soulfully and romantically? Slow and leisurely? Light and tickly? "Listen" to what her body is telling you. Notice the rhythm at which she touches you; it may well be the rhythm at which she likes to be touched. If you feel you just aren't getting her message physically, be brave and ask her verbally. Don't be shy. Just whisper sexily into her ear something to the effect of, "How does this feel? . . . Do you like that?" Tease her. Bring her close to orgasm and then pull back, slow down, lessen stimulation, and then start over. This gradual buildup of sexual energy, increasing and decreasing excitement through teasing, will result in more spectacular orgasms for both of you.

Find Her Special Pleasure Points

Explore the sensual paradise of her body. Be creative in your approach. *Don't* make a beeline for her nipples or genitalia, unless you know her well and it's *not* something you usually do. *Do* pay special attention to her personal, physical, extragenital pleasure points wherever you find them (see Lady's Commandment #2: Thou Shalt Stimulate Her Senses, page 11): in her feet, her fingers, her ears, the nape of her neck, the small of her back, the inside of her elbow, the curve of her underarm, the corridors of her mind.

Every woman is potentially orgasmic in at least one part of her body that is technically not a "sex organ."

If she says she's not in the mood for sex, try simply stroking and rubbing her hand. Sometimes, when Max rubs my hand, he can take me from not-in-the-mood to in-the-mood within minutes (I don't know how many minutes, because when Max is rubbing my hand like that, I lose track of time).

T&A

Now it might be time to play with her beautiful breasts. When in doubt, play it soft. Though some women go wild over rough breast play (even "nipple torture"), many have sensitive breasts and complain that men "grab" them coarsely or fiddle with their nipples like dials on an old-fashioned radio. Use finesse in handling these tender delicacies, whether they're big or small.

Her buns are probably a lot tougher. If she's like me and most other ladies I know, you can grab, squeeze, and spank her ass practically to your heart's content, and she'll love it. Careful around her anus, though. It can be a major pleasure point for some ladies (and gentlemen), but due to various physical and psychological factors, a lot of women have uptight assholes! When in doubt around the anal area, play that foreplay light, slow, well lubricated, and indirect.

Pet the Kitty (with Your Tongue)

And now we come to what the Taoists call her "gates of heaven," what the Tantrists called her *yoni*, her sacred space, her wondrous vulva, her mound of Venus, her cunny, her cunt, her kitty, her (I hope by this point) steaming-wet *pussy*. A subcommandment here should be: Thou Shalt Lick Her Pussy.

The bonobos do it, and you can, too. Lubricate your lips and liberate your homeland! Stretch out your tongue and get ready to lick, lap, and love it! Many ladies can only have orgasms through oral sex, or as the Latins call it, cunnilingus (from *cunnus:* vulva and *lingus:* tongue), because this way, the clitoris and labia can be stimulated directly but oh-so-very gently and sweetly, releasing her luscious vaginal "honey."

There are many aspects to the art of cunnilingus (or as one of my lady sex therapy clients puts it: to being a "cunning linguist"), but it is most important *to act like you're enjoying it*. This is so that the lady you're licking doesn't feel that you're doing her a favor, which induces in her a sense of guilt, inhibiting her pleasure. The easiest way to act like you're enjoying it is to really enjoy it. And the best way to really enjoy it is to get good at it. If you suspect you might not be so good at it, you may want to take this tip from the late great comedian Sam Kinison, who explained his cunnilingus technique on my radio show:

> *Once you've got your lady in the proper position for maximum*
> *receptivity, carefully write out every letter*
> *of the alphabet—with your tongue.*

It works. You should have her screaming by the time you get to P! Sam seemed to do pretty well with it; he was always surrounded by beautiful women even before he got rich and famous. And he looked like a human troll doll. Just goes to show: A good sense of humor and the ability to tongue your ABCs goes a long, long way with the ladies.

Moist and Juicy
Baseball player Phil Garner put it like this, "You have to do to tobacco like you do to women. You must let it work up to a good chew, let it get moist and juicy. If you chew too fast, it will become dry and fall apart." You might want to keep a glass of water nearby to wet your whistle. Ice is also fun. Roll a piece of ice around in your mouth and then lick and suck away. Turns cunnilingus into sipping a cooool drink—a vaginal slurpy!

Go on, slurp her up, dive into her ocean, swim through her warm, thick currents, and make your way home.

Pearl Diving

The center of a lady's pleasure is her clitoris (see Lady's Commandment #4: Thou Shalt Encourage Her to Show and Tell You How She Likes to Be Touched, page 32), little Miss Clitty, the precious pearl of her luscious oyster, that cute Little Red Riding Hood centrally located toward the top of the vulva just over the entrance to the vagina (hey, lots of guys and some women don't know where the clitoris is, so I thought I'd get a little geography in here).

In a purely physical sense, her clitoris—the most intense pleasure point of her body—is the key to her Holy Grail.

Lick it, flick it, suck it, finger it, tap it, stroke it, spank it lightly, play with it, feel how it grows between your lips or against your fingertips, try new things with it, and vary your tongue and finger movements, always paying very close attention to her particular responses. These responses are signals that tell you how she likes what you're doing. For instance, if her legs open up or her tummy distends or her back arches, pushing her vulva toward your mouth, or if she moans, "Yes! yes! yes!", you know you're doing something right. Pay attention to her breathing: it should set the rhythm of your tongue movement. When in doubt, just *ask* what she likes, as in, "Do you like that?" (*lick, lap, slurp*). . . . "How about like this?" (*lap, lap, suck, nibble*), though if she's enjoying it, don't be surprised if she squeezes her thighs around your head and hisses, "Ooohhhhh . . . just shut up and suck!"

Remember, every lady is different. Some like direct clitoral stimulation, some prefer for you to focus your licking just above, below, or to the side of her clitoris. Most prefer that you lick first, slowly lapping up and down, not quite licking her clit or her anus or penetrating her labia, *then* suck, then nibble. When she's already nice and juiced up, try holding her clit between two fingers and slurping her into ecstasy.

A lady's clitoral desires tend to change with her mood and the time of month; be sensitive to that. Whatever you do, keep it wet. The wetter the clitoris is, the more aroused it is, and the more vigorously you can devour it. Do not try to greedily gobble a dry clit, or you may find yourself on the receiving end of a swift kick in the solar plexus. Remember: *lubrication, lubrication, lubrication!*

Make her clit swell and strain for your tongue, make her vulva open up and "beg" for you to enter. Try holding your mouth still, letting her rub up against you. When you feel she's ready, let your tongue dive in between her labia, down into her heated pool, her warm and salty sea. As you can see, you can do a lot to arouse her before entering her vagina with your tongue, let alone your fingers or penis.

> *Remember: the vulva is the door to her pleasure,*
> *and the clitoris is the doorbell.*

A gentleman doesn't forget to ring a lady's doorbell before he enters her pleasure palace.

It's the Vulva, Stupid!

For all his brilliance and originality in other areas, Dr. Sigmund Freud, father of psychoanalysis, was a major doofus regarding female sexual anatomy. Freud said that while the erotic center of *young girls* is the clitoris (the central pleasure point of the vulva), as girls mature into *women*, sexual excitation must be transferred to the vagina. That is, a "mature" woman has vaginal orgasms, not clitoral orgasms. So convinced was Dr. Freud of the correspondence between mature sexuality and vaginal eroticism that he maintained that "the elimination of clitoridal sexuality is a necessary precondition for the development of femininity," and he defined frigidity as the inability to make the "orgasmic transfer" from clitoris to vagina.[1] And boy, did that make a lot of perfectly orgasmic women feel like total horsepuckey.

But, never fear, Dr. Alfred Kinsey became our sexual knight in shining armor, a troubadour in a white lab coat. "There is," Dr. Kinsey wrote, "no evidence that the vagina is ever the sole source of arousal . . . in any female."[2] The female vulva, which includes the clitoris, is the orgasmic epicenter of every woman. Sometimes, a woman feels the orgasm vibrating deep inside her vagina but a wet, well-rubbed, happy vulva is still the entrance of her pleasure, and if you don't have the key, you don't get in. Well, you can get in, but you wouldn't be very welcome.

[1] Sigmund Freud, "Some Psychological Consequences of the Anatomical Distinction Between the Sexes" (1925), in *Standard Edition of the Complete Psychological Works*. Vol. XIX, trans. and ed. James Strachey (London: Hogarth Press, 1961), p. 191.
[2] Alfred Kinsey, *Sexual Behavior in the Human Female* (Philadelphia: W. B. Saunders, 1953), p. 582.

You must touch the vulva to trigger orgasm.

Wu Hu!
Empress Wu Hu, who ruled China during the T'ang Dynasty, had the right idea when she decreed that all government officials and visiting dignitaries must pay homage to her Imperial Highness by performing cunnilingus upon her. Really! Old paintings depict the beautiful, powerful empress standing and holding her ornate robe open, while a high official, nobleman, or diplomat is shown kneeling humbly before her, lavishly applying his lips and tongue to her royal netherparts. . . .

Shouldn't your lady be so honored by you, her noble man?

Be Patient
Remember: the distaff tends to be slower to arouse. A couple of laps and a peck on her inner thigh won't cut it. Ladies often complain that guys simply don't eat them long enough to get their juices flowing, let alone bring them to a climax. Jackie, one of my sex therapy clients, was constantly frustrated because her husband didn't lick her for more than a few seconds before he was climbing on top to enter her. I suggested she switch positions and sit on his face. Now she won't let him get up until she's good and ready!

Of course, not every lady is bold enough for face-sitting. If your lady prefers to lie back and receive cunnilingus, it's up to you to keep lapping for as long as she needs. Eat your favorite food from between her legs if it helps you to stay down there long enough to give your lady pleasure! Seriously, try honey, chocolate mousse, whipped cream, soy sauce, champagne, guacamole—whatever turns on your taste buds and keeps you licking.

Remember how you "developed a taste" for certain vegetables when you were little? Well, if you haven't already, it's time for you to develop a taste for something carnal: *pussy!* It may be sweet and sour, musky and flowery, or fishy and salty. Like fine French cuisine, when prepared correctly, it's always saucy.

G-Spot Hunting
While you lick her, try sliding your finger inside of her just up to the first knuckle, then the second knuckle, then a second finger. Maybe

three fingers (check her signals). Maybe four. Slowly wiggle your fingers around in there. Feel her wet, spongy vaginal walls pulsating with pleasure. You might be able to feel her G spot; your fingers can touch it in a way that a penis can't.[3] Inside, move your finger in a "come-here" gesture. When your finger curls up and back toward you, you'll feel an area against the back of her pubic bone, like a spongy, sort of corrugated, soft bump under the roof of her vaginal cave. Stroke it gently. Vary the movement. Try rubbing, tapping, pressing, vibrating, swirling. Now go deeper, maybe faster, maybe harder. Suck her clit with gusto. Tongue her ass if you're bold, and she's game.

WARNING: Touching her G spot may hurt, it may tickle, it may feel weird or wonderful. It may make her orgasm. It may even make her ejaculate. When you touch it, you must be ready to deal with whatever it releases.

Use Your Tool

Now what about your penis, your mighty manroot? I haven't forgotten it. How could I? I just want to make sure that you use it to give her pleasure. Don't worry, we'll get to *its* pleasure in Gentleman's Commandment #2: Thou Shalt Adore His Penis (page 94). And sometimes you should have sex primarily for the pleasure of your penis. But other times, you should use your penis primarily to give your partner pleasure. Try it. You may be surprised at how exciting it is for everybody, including Mr. Willy.

Before you penetrate her with it, rub it against her. Tease her with it. Let her play with it. Don't enter her until she's begging for it, or at least until she asks for it in some way. *Sometimes* a fast hard plunge inside is just what a lady craves. But more often than not she prefers a slow, gradual entry. You might want to linger with just the head inside. That's a delicious feeling.

You can never go wrong by letting her put "peter" in her.

---

[3]Ernst von Grafenberg, a German physician, is said to have "discovered" the G Spot, which he named after himself. Some experts say that the G spot doesn't exist. All I can say is that *I* have one, as do most ladies I know.

Now it's in. You're in! But whoa, boy. Just because you're in doesn't mean no more foreplay. Now let foreplay become more play. This is a good time for a passionate kiss, an intimate hug, a warm caress, a sensual nipple twist, maybe a hot slap on the butt, perhaps a lusty or romantic phrase whispered in her ear, depending on her personal pleasure points. It sounds corny, but it's good to keep this in mind: *Don't just fuck her, make love to her.* Unless you've already made love to her a few dozen times. Then a nice hot fuck might do you both good.

Don't Get Lost in the Forest

Of course, fucking and making love both can take countless different forms. There are so many positions—missionary, woman-on-top, doggy-style, spoon-style, yabyum- or yogi-style, zen- or tantric-style.[4] Find out which positions and styles really stimulate her physical and mental pleasure points.

> *Whatever position you get into, don't get lost in the forest*
> *and neglect Little Red Riding Hood.*

Since her clitoris is on the outside, it can dry up even when she's all juiced up inside, *if* you don't keep it wet and well rubbed. Just lick your finger—or let her lick your finger, or her finger (remember: mutual pleasure is a team effort)—and rub it every few strokes. Then you can have fun trying to find her G spot again, this time with the head of your cock.

Hopefully, your lady will have her orgasm before yours ("ladies first" is a good rule of thumb, or tongue, as the case may be), but if she doesn't, that's okay, too. Just keep things going, with your semi-hard penis, your tongue, fingers, a dildo, a vibrator, whatever presses her pleasure points—until she does. It's a good idea to have a dildo or vibrator around as a "backup system," in case your hard-drive/hard-on "goes down."

> *You have backup systems for your computer,*
> *shouldn't you have one for your sex life?*

---

[4]Zen- or tantric-style sex generally involves spending long periods of time with your penis inside her, but motionless, without thrusting, breathing together and feeling the energy move between you both, meditating on the meaning of your union.

What If She Can't Come?

If for some reason, she simply can't have an orgasm, do not pressure her. Remember: *Pressure is the enemy of pleasure.*

Don't get me wrong: Orgasm is plenty pleasurable. If your female primemate is pre-orgasmic, that is, if she has never been able to have an orgasm, you and she may wish to get help from an expert. In the meantime, turn her on to deep oceanic breathing and the fabulous, unisex PC muscle exercise (see Gentleman's Commandment #2: Thou Shalt Adore His Penis, page 94). Some perfectly orgasmic ladies, however, do not climax with every sexual encounter. Orgasm is wonderful, but not always absolutely necessary to a lady's pleasure. Nothing is absolute when it comes to sexual pleasure. Even the most orgasmic of women have times when it just won't "come," and if you try to push it, you'll only wind up irritating her mentally and physically.

Female Ejaculation
Some ladies actually ejaculate with orgasm. A buttery fluid that some experts say is diluted urine, but others say is more like a somewhat stronger brew of vaginal honey, what the tantrics call *amrita* ("nectar of the goddess") can come spurting out of the urethra as she climaxes. Some ladies can ejaculate clear across a room. If you'd like to see whether you can help your lady to spurt, suggest she do PC muscle exercises and deep breathing on a regular basis. Then, when you're both in the mood for a little geyser of love, tease her a lot, bringing her just to the brink of orgasm and back down again several times. Then finger her G spot and spank her clit. Experiment. If you get spritzed, you'll know she spurted. If not, don't worry about it. Most ladies can't, or at least haven't been able to, have this sort of climax.

Going for Numbers
How about multiple orgasms? Why not double, triple, or quadruple her pleasure? Some lucky ladies have multiple orgasms with ease, some don't. For many women, one nice big one per encounter is plenty.

Keep in mind that giving a lady multiple orgasms, or even one orgasm, has as much to do with her capacity to receive pleasure as it does with your ability to give it.

But if you and she want to go for the numbers, just keep flowing from foreplay to more play. Deep breathing and strong PC muscles help a lot, but *you* can help too by varying your approaches to each of her orgasms. Since orgasms don't necessarily follow a logical progression, you and your primemate should develop your own flexible series of climactic delights.

That said, you might want to try this Multiple Orgasm Stimulation Sequence: Start by giving her a purely clitoral orgasm from oral sex, with nothing more than a finger or two inside her. Remember that after a big orgasm, many ladies need a recovery period of anywhere from five seconds to fifteen minutes (during which time you'd better not touch her clit or you might get hit!), though some women can enjoy a string of climaxes, one right after the other, in a continuous stream of ecstatic pleasure. The next orgasm you give your lady could be through light penetration, with just about half of your passion-packed love machine throbbing inside her, rubbing and wetting little Miss Clitty all the while, caressing, squeezing, or spanking your lady's other physical pleasure points wherever you find them, and stimulating her mental pleasure points by whispering an erotic fantasy, words of love, or hot dirty talk into her ear. For a third climax, slowly but surely slide your cock all the way in, heating up the action, maybe squeezing her nipples or slipping a wet finger up the crack of her ass. For a fourth, thrust in and out with hard pumping penetration, really giving it to her, hitting up against that G spot, continuing to juice up her clit. Then change positions, going from missionary to woman-on-top or doggy-style or whatever position you can get your bodies into, for a fifth orgasm. Then bring in the heavy artillery—a vibrator—one of those nice big massager "magic wands" that can almost always pull a climax out of any clit, and you may be able to give her one, two, or three more. But if you get that far, chances are you'll have both lost count!

Recommended Reading
Blank, Joani. *Good Vibrations: The Complete Guide to Vibrators*. San Francisco: Down There Press, 1982.
Brauer, Alan J., and Donna Brauer. *ESO (Expanded Sexual Orgasm)*. New York: Warner Books, 1989.

Comfort, Alex. *The New Joy of Sex*. New York: Crown Publishers, 1991.

Hite, Shere. *The Hite Report*. New York: Macmillan, 1976.

Hooper, Anne. *The Ultimate Sex Book*. New York: Dorling Kindersley, 1992.

Keesling, Barbara. *How to Make Love All Night: And Drive a Woman Wild*. New York: HarperCollins, 1995.

Ladas, Alice. *The G Spot and Other Recent Discoveries About Human Sexuality*. New York: Holt, Rinehart & Winston, 1982.

Ogden, Gina. *Women Who Love Sex*, ed. Denise Silvestro. New York: Simon & Schuster, 1994.

10

THOU SHALT

Find Out What Her Dreams

Are Made Of . . .

. . . and help her to realize them, even if that means just talking to her about them.

> *Help your primemate to explore, understand, and actualize*
> *her dreams, her hopes, her ambitions, her fantasies.*

Her Fantasies Are Her Freedom

A lady's fantasies are always with her, always playing hide-and-seek with what seems to be reality, whispering wild ideas into her inner ear, showing movies in her mind, stirring her passions mysteriously yet so powerfully. If she is imprisoned in any way—by her work, her marriage, her government, her upbringing, her situation—her fantasies become her freedom. Sometimes her ability to fantasize is the only freedom she has.

Support Her Ambitions
Support the dreams and fantasies that involve her life goals, her career, her causes, and concerns. When she's discouraged, try to comfort, reassure, and revitalize her. If you're in a position to help her

fulfill her dreams, don't hold back. Get her jobs, if you can. Put her in films if you make them. Help her with her homework. Assist her in strategizing meetings. Read her manuscripts. At least, be a good listener to her tales of working woe and triumph. Get involved with her life. Get on her team, learn to play all the positions. Always remind her of the big picture, that she's great and deserves the best.

Everybody has a gift, a talent for doing something, whether it's being a genetic biophysicist, a stripper, or a homemaker. Help her to discover her gift by exploring her dreams. Help her to evolve into the highest form of human being she can be. If you don't get interested in her work—if you don't give her the pleasure of your support— someone else will, probably someone at work. That's one reason why passionate office affairs are so popular.

> *There's nothing like mixing a little business with pleasure*
> *to create erotic heat.*

If *you* ignore her work life, she'll eventually be cozying up to someone who doesn't.

That goes for all kinds of work, including "domestic engineering." If you and she have kids together, raise them together. If the kids are hers, help her where she clearly asks for help.

Discover Her Dreams Before You Fall (Too Deeply) in Love

This is not an easy commandment to follow. What if her dreams or fantasies threaten yours? With love and trust, you may be able to get over feeling threatened. But if you can't get over it, and you stay together anyway, you will cause each other more pain than pleasure. That's why it's so important to talk to her about her dreams *before* you fall in love. If it's love at first sight, well then, better talk fast!

Remember: She's the Boss

She's in charge of her dreams and fantasies. She's the head honcho of *her* life. But you can help. You *should* help, if you want to give her pleasure. Unless she tells you she doesn't want your help. But if she doesn't want your help, that's a pretty clear signal that she doesn't really want you.

Do Ladies Have Sexual Fantasies?

Yes, of course they do, and they always have, ever since Eve enticed Adam to eat her . . . apple.[1] The only thing new about female sexual fantasies is that now ladies are more open about discussing them. Encourage your primemate to tell you her fantasies. She may not tell you all of them, at least, not at once. You needn't rush to find out *all* her dreams; "the goal is the journey" in your search for her Holy Grail. But the more you explore her fantasies, the more exciting your relationship will be.

Experience Two Kinds of Sex at Once
We humans are animals in many ways, especially when it comes to sex. But *unlike* other animals, we can communicate complex ideas through *speech*. That ability lets us have two kinds of sex at once. For instance, you could have straight one-on-one intercourse in reality, a wild orgy in fantasy. Through whispering fantasies into each other's ears during sex, or during phone sex, you can experience all kinds of adventures you couldn't or wouldn't act out, and you can learn your primemate's fantasies. They may be romantic, orgiastic, tender or wild. Since many fantasies involve turning the status quo on its ear, they can also be quite shocking. Even frightening. I told you that the path to her Holy Grail had creatures of her past leaping across it. These are her fantasies. Don't be afraid; it's only a dream you are in.

*Don't Make Like the Thought Police and Bust Her
for Her Fantasies*
Don't hold her dreams against her. You can hold her responsible for her actions, not her thoughts. Then, again, if she's having recurring fantasies of chopping you up and making you into barbecue for her ladies luncheon group, and if she just bought a jumbo grill, you ought to get the hell out now! Unless you really love her. *Just kidding.* There are crazy, violent women out there (nowhere near as many as there are crazy, violent men, but if one of the few is your wife, and

---

[1]Of course, *that* was a male fantasy, probably composed by a bunch of horny ancient Hebrew scribes.

she's throwing a bottle at your head, statistics don't much matter), so if you're with one, better slip out the back, Jack, if you value your life.

Coax Out Her Dreams

Assuming she's not an ice pick murderer or chronic bottle thrower, encourage your primemate to tell you her fantasies. The female is rarely encouraged to articulate her raw desires. Ladies in our society hardly ever have the experience of paying for sex and getting "whatever you want" as so many men do. Women are not taught to think of this as even a possibility for them. Ask her what kind of sex she'd be willing to pay for—if she had the money, if it was totally safe, if no one would think badly of her, and if she could get whatever she wanted.

Romance, Pornography, and the Fetish for Love

To find out more about the fantasies that give her pleasure, sneak a peek at what she likes to read to relax. Any romance novels? Conventional wisdom is that male erotica is pornography and female erotica is romance. This is true *to some extent*. Just as billions of dollars each year come out of mostly men's pockets to support the pornography industry, so every year, billions of dollars are spent on romance novels—almost all from women. Just goes to show that male and female sexual fantasies are totally different, right? Well, not exactly. Upon close examination, one sees that these two seemingly disparate forms of erotic expression have quite a bit in common.

If your lady is into romance novels, take a good look at one. You'll probably be surprised at how lusty it is, how it drips with fantasy worlds, erotic tension, and lots of actual "bodice-ripping" sex. As in "male" pornography, in "female" romance, the main characters are idealized, gorgeous, sexual superhumans. All the women are multiply orgasmic, though most start out as virgins, and all the men are long-lasting erotic athletes. Neither genre is terribly "deep"—we're not talking great literature in either case. In romance, as in pornography, there are scenes of exhibitionism and voyeurism, scenes of dominance and submission, scenes of passionate, unbridled sex suffused with danger. Both genres include fetish scenes that eroticize articles of clothing such as shoes, leather, and tight corsets. The main difference between "male" pornography and "female" romance, and this is the crux of the matter, is *love*. In romance, the hero and heroine *must* fall in love, and usually they get married in the end. In pornography, love is not an issue, and marriage is about as relevant as doing laundry (less, in fact; more porn scenes are set in Laundromats than at weddings).

The Female Fetish for Love

The most popular female fetish is the fetish for LOVE. How can love be considered a "fetish"? A fetish is something that is technically *unnecessary* to the sexual act that the fetishist needs in order to perform (male) or enjoy (female) the sexual act. Love is not necessary to the sexual act, any more than high heels or leather (typical "fetish" items) are necessary to the sexual act, and yet many people, especially women, can't or won't have sex without love or, at least, the possibility of love.

If that sounds like your lady, you know she has a love fetish. You know that it is vital to her erotic nature that you dramatically demonstrate your love to her, that you shower her with tokens of love, that you say, "I love you," often. If all of this seems syrupy to you, get over it! Or get over her. Love is what gets her hot.

Make Romance
Read one of her romance novels, then ask her what she thinks of certain scenes. You may never be mistaken for a romantic hero, just as she'll probably never be a porn star, but you can do romantic things. You can "sweep her off her feet" (if she's not built like a minivan), you can dance with her (if you can't dance, *learn*), you can imbue your relationship with special meaning, and you can follow these commandments. Just *trying* to follow them will turn you into quite a romantic creature.

Other Common Female Fetishes and Fantasies[2]

Some Enchanted Evening
One of the most popular sex fantasies—male or female—is seduction of or by an exciting stranger. Now please, PC Police, I do *not* recom-

[2]For more popular erotic fantasies and fetishes, see Gentleman's Commandment #7: Thou Shalt Discover His Deepest Desires and Fantasies (pp. 141–156).

mend *actual* seduction of or by a stranger, no matter how exciting. Not in real life, at least not without sheathing your entire body in a suit of latex spermicidal armor, *the* shining armor of the Knight of the 1990s. But the *fantasy* of seduction of or by a stranger is a delightful aphrodisiac that many ladies (and gentlemen) do enjoy, and there's nothing wrong with that.

> No matter how committed we are to wholesome, familiar
> "family values," we will always find something erotic about
> the unfamiliar, the strange, the mysterious,
> the potentially dangerous, and very romantic unknown.

One of my favorite fantasies is to pretend that Max, who I'm *very* familiar with, is a handsome stranger. Maybe he plays the role of one of my fans who listens to all my shows or someone applying to work for me. We pretend that "my husband's away," then I seduce him or he seduces me. That way, we can have a wild night of passion with a mysterious, forbidden outlaw, a stranger, and wake up with each other!

Bisexual Fantasies

It's very common for outwardly "straight" ladies to dream of having sex with other ladies. As Dr. Alfred Kinsey was among the first to point out, we're all on a sort of bisexual continuum with absolute heterosexuals on one end and total homosexuals on the other end.[3] Very few, if any, of us fall at one end or the other. Most of us are bisexual to some degree. That doesn't usually mean we like both sexes equally. It just means most of us can potentially be aroused by anyone, regardless of gender. Erotic philosopher Gore Vidal put it this way: "There is no such thing as a homosexual or a heterosexual person. There are only homo- or heterosexual acts. Most people are a mixture of impulses if not practices."[4]

When Pulitzer Prize–winning poet Edna St. Vincent Millay went to a doctor for her recurrent headaches, and he suggested that they

---

[3]June M. Reinisch, *The Kinsey Institute New Report on Sex*, rev. ed. (New York: St. Martin's Press, 1990), p. 140.
[4]Gore Vidal, "Tennessee Williams: Someone to Laugh at the Squares With," in *At Home: Essays 1982–1988* (New York: Random House, 1988).

might stem from "an occasional erotic impulse toward a person of [her] own sex," Millay responded, "Oh, you mean I'm homosexual? Of course, I am, and heterosexual too, but what's that got to do with my headache?"[5]

If your lady is having bisexual "impulses" or fantasies, it could mean that she actually wants to have a sexual experience with another woman. Then, again, it could suggest that she's getting more in touch with her own sexuality, accepting or searching for the power and pleasure of her femaleness. It can also mean that she needs some tenderness in her life, some nurturing female energy that she doesn't necessarily have to get from an actual woman (hopefully, she can get it from you).

Talk to her about her bisexual fantasies. This can be a great turn-on for both of you when you're making love. If you're comfortable with *your* female side, you might want to role-play that you're two ladies in bed together. Otherwise, you can be the male voyeur watching her frolic with another woman.

If the idea of seeing her with another woman turns you on too, you *might* ask her if this is something she'd like to explore in real life. If she says no, she wants to keep it in the realm of fantasy, do *not* push her. Remember: *pressure is the enemy of pleasure*. If she's interested in actually having sex with a woman, you may want to talk about how you can arrange it so that everyone is as safe and happy as possible— though with three variable humans, nothing is certain. Keep in mind that sharing your bed with a third person is a big step that you and she may never be ready for, no matter how wild your fantasies.

> *In fantasy, everything is perfect. In reality, some people don't get along, other people get jealous, and body parts don't all work right.*

You might want to try an interim measure, such as going to a lesbian bar and watching her as she dances sensually with some sexy ladies. Or try calling a phone sex line together, so she can experience talking erotically with another woman without having to deal with her actual presence in your bed. Or, just continue to talk and think and dream about it for a while . . . After all, what's the rush?

[5]Irving Wallace, *The Intimate Sex Lives of Famous People* (London: Arrow Books, 1981), p. 304.

Watching and Being Watched

Perhaps the lady in your life wants to explore exhibitionism and voyeurism, seeing and being seen, showing off and watching the show. As you learned under Lady's Commandment #3: Thou Shalt Compliment Her Meaningfully and Often (page 27), the human female often has a streak of exhibitionism. And modern Western society does encourage her to be sexy, if not actually sexual. Marilyn Monroe is said to have had recurring dreams in which she stripped off all her clothes in church as a stunned congregation silently worshipped her naked beauty.[6] Most ladies wouldn't go that far (even Marilyn kept her nude appearances to secular venues in real life), but many do love to show off.

If that sounds like your primemate, try not to be threatened by her exhibitionism. Just think of her as a beautiful flower blooming in your own backyard. Why would you pick that flower, take it inside, and cover it up? If you're struggling with feelings of embarrassment and fear over her exhibitionist tendencies, try to understand and deal with them rationally, instead of lashing out at her or telling her she looks like a "slut." As long as she's not wearing or doing anything that'll get her arrested or in some other kind of trouble, try supporting her in her erotic self-expression. Try being proud of how sexy she is. If you stop and think about it, you might realize that you ought to be proud. And consider this: If you try to squelch her, you will only lose her, one way or another.

If she's more of a voyeur, and many people are both, well, lucky you! You get to show off for her. In our society, we tend to think of exhibitionism as female and voyeurism as male. After all, most strip clubs have female strippers, male customers. The great majority of straight-sex magazines have pictures of women for men to look at. Most people would say this is natural, but is it? In nature, it's usually the male of the species that's the exhibitionist, the classic example being the peacock, strutting his sexual stuff for the female who watches him voyeuristically, deciding whether he'd make a good sex partner.

Try stripping and strutting for her. Keep it light and fun (see Lady's Commandment #6: Thou Shalt Make Her Laugh, page 45). She just

[6]Ibid., p. 310.

might love it; I love to watch Max or other gentlemen show off for me. As the power dynamic between female and male changes in our society, and it *is* changing, it will be interesting to see how our concepts of exhibitionism and voyeurism change to match. . . .

Surrender and Power Trips

Power and surrender, or dominance and submission (D&S) fantasies are also common. Both ladies and gentlemen of all different kinds of upbringings have them. Actually, they're even older than the human race. They can be crude or romantic, marvelous or dangerous. Fantasies may involve body worship, spanking, whipping, tickling, sadomasochism (SM), bondage and discipline (B&D), and a host of other activities that may or may not involve actual sexual intercourse.

NOTE: Many people are alarmed by the images evoked by a discussion of D&S, SM, and B&D fantasies. I support the safe, consensual exploration of these fantasies as a way for some people to peacefully channel violent impulses. This can serve as a sexually psychodramatic stage in the process of safely releasing and bringing to consciousness aggressive forces that often lurk in the unconscious where they can be more dangerous. It may even help to decrease domestic violence. An in-depth discussion of this subject is way beyond the scope of these commandments. If that's what you're looking for, there are plenty of good books on D&S, B&D, and SM, especially those of San Francisco Bay Area writer Pat Califia (see Recommended Reading).

Female Domination

If your lady is interested in exploring her sexual power, you may want to find ways in which you enjoy being her "love slave," "boy toy," "pet dog," "baby bonobo," "prisoner of love," or whatever submissive role fits your personality and her desire. Max plays, among other roles, my "butler." Much of the time, he treats me like an empress, waits on me, worships my body, lets me "use" him for my pleasure, shoots my videos, and assists me in running my mini-empire. Notice I say "much of the time." Most good long-term relationships are flexible, not locked into one dominant/submissive dynamic. Partners "switch" dominant and submissive roles depending on mood, circumstances, and other factors.

Part of the current feminist-sexual revolution involves women getting in touch with the pleasure and responsibility of wielding sexual power, something which men have had a virtual monopoly on in the past. Experimenting with female dominance and male submission brings into the open the power imbalances that have for millennia characterized sexual relations.

So c'mon, be a sport, let her ride you, spank your ass, strap on a dildo and do to you what you usually do to her! Seriously, you might be surprised at how much you enjoy being on the receiving end of aggressive sex.

Many ladies like the erotic rush of sexual power; some just prefer to get what they want when they want it. Some may want to "get back" at fathers, brothers, and ex-lovers who dominated them in the past. One of my clients, Claire, was physically abused by her stepfather from the age of seven to sixteen, and when she grew up, she found it difficult to relax and enjoy sex. She was passive, inorgasmic, barely able to tolerate intercourse. Then a new boyfriend told her he didn't want to have sex in the typical way. He wanted to worship her, to submit to her power, to follow her sexual orders. At first, she was alarmed by his suggestions (that's when she first came to see me), but she was also intrigued. Besides, she liked this new guy a lot. She trusted him. She decided to try being "dominant," and found herself feeling comfortable with sex for the first time. The feeling of control relaxed her and allowed her to experience orgasm as she never had before. Knowing that she, not the male, was in charge—that sex could be whatever she wanted it to be—helped her to lift the heavy burden of fear and loathing she'd been carrying since she was a helpless little girl, and virtually toss it out the window!

While the typical male dominant enjoys penis worship, the female generally desires full body worship, starting with the feet, the lowest part of her body. She may also enjoy administering "punishment," or just treating her lover like a "sex object." For more on domination, see Gentleman's Commandment #7: Thou Shalt Discover His Deepest Desires and Fantasies (pages 147–148).

CAUTION: Whether you're male or female, or that special something in between, don't do anything you're really uncomfortable with just to please your partner. There's nothing uncool about saying you're not ready for something or explaining your discomfort so that you can change or adapt what you're doing and make it comfortable. Just don't call your primemate "weirdo" names for sharing her fantasies with you, unless you don't mind losing her completely.

Female Submission

Perhaps your primemate wants to explore her submissive side. Most of the 10 Commandments of a Lady's Pleasure help you to serve *her* pleasure, but she may genuinely enjoy pleasing you. Tell her to study the 10 Commandments of a Gentleman's Pleasure, and test her mercilessly.

Being submissive is, of course, the more traditional feminine sex role, but she may enjoy it for rather nontraditional reasons. In love (as opposed to war, politics, or business, where "surrender" conjures visions of defeat and shame), surrender is sweet and the ultimate intimate fulfillment.

> *Since society puts so much pressure on all of us—male and female—to be powerful, to achieve, to succeed, deep in our erotic imaginations, many of us may long to surrender.*

Your lady may feel that surrendering to someone she loves and trusts (that's you!), someone she knows truly loves and trusts her, gives her tremendous power. She may feel powerful, not weak, as she enjoys the fantasy of a sexy gentleman tying her up and ravishing her; after all, in her fantasy, she is so desirable that the gentleman cannot resist her.

> *The ancient Taoist masters had a saying,*
> *"In yielding, there is strength."*
> *In surrender, there can be power.*
> *In restraint, there can be freedom.*

Keep in mind if you are physically playing out D&S fantasies that it may seem like the dominant partner is in control, but the reality should be that the submissive partner's threshold of pain is in con-

trol. If your lady likes to be submissive, you must pay even more attention to the details of her desire *and* well-being.

Her submissive desires may involve a rape, ravishment, or abduc-
tion fantasy. Partly because our society is so negative about sex, many
women and men fantasize about being forced against their will to
have sex. That way, they don't feel so responsible, and can just relax
and enjoy it. Now, of course, just because a woman—or anyone—has
a rape fantasy does *not* mean she really wants to be raped. *No* woman
really wants to be raped. No man does either, but lots of men fantasize about it.

*Remember, a little fear and danger spice sex up, but not too much
now, and always present a fearful fantasy or an aggressive maneuver with love, never cruelty.*

Ravishment fantasies often involve bondage, or as the French call
it, *ligottage*, the gentle art of tying up your sex partner—with anything from storm trooper–style handcuffs to an old pair of nylons—
the purpose being *not* to literally force your lover to do something
they're truly frightened of or don't want to do, but to heighten excitement by mutually creating the erotic *illusion* of fear and force.
Consensuality is the key to this delicate erotic art, the sensual science of restraint. Politically incorrect as it is, a great many sexual
acts between humans, as well as other animals, involve one partner
restraining the other.

If you think people into bondage are weird, consider the common
wedding ring, still one of our great symbols of *human bondage*. And
bonding is a kind of bondage, isn't it? Commitment is a kind of restraint. Love is a kind of silken rope that ties two people together.
Simply being held tight and close in the arms of someone we love is
a confinement we all adore. In a way, bondage games take bonding to
the outer erotic limits. . . .

Many lovers wear masks, not just on Halloween, but any time they
want to appear menacingly sexy, other than themselves, possessed by
the mask. Masks are one of the very oldest human devices for con-
juring mystical and sexual inspiration. . . . Not just kid stuff, after all.

*Next time you're in bed, and you feel like wearing a mask but
don't have one handy, just put your lady's panties over your head.
This can be funny or scary, and most aromatic. . . .*

Good Girl/Bad Girl

She might also like playing the role of the "little girl." That generally puts you in the role of "Daddy." Depending on her relationship with her own father or primary male caretaker, she might enjoy being "made" to show off for "Daddy," spanked (not too hard now!) for being a "bad girl" or praised for being a "good girl." Little girl fantasies go beyond submissive roles. We all love acting like a kid again for a variety of reasons (see Gentleman's Commandment #8: Thou Shalt Remember What Thy Mama Said, "All Men Are Little Boys," page 157). In her "little girl" mode, she might enjoy being a dominant, bratty, bossy, little bitch. Then, again, she may not want you to be dominant or submissive, but just to be another little kid with her, talking babytalk, tickling each other, being silly, playing with child-like abandon.

Bonobo (and Other Animal) Fantasies

Her wild erotic nature may emerge in animal-sex fantasies. Don't worry, having animal-sex fantasies doesn't (usually) mean your primemate actually wants to have sex with an animal. She may just like the bestial wildness. She may fantasize that you're a horse (ladies love horses), or that she's a leopard (why do you think those leopard-print bikinis are always so popular?). Or you can both be bonobo chimpanzees, jumping all over each other, wrestling playfully in your jungle of sheets and pillows.

Sacred Sex

Your primemate's sexual fantasies could be spiritual. She might see you as an angel with wings to take her flying. She might think of your sexual union as a spiritual, cosmic merger of two souls becoming one. You can set the sexual scene for your cosmic lady with lots of candles, incense, crystals, spiritual music (try Gregorian chants, Tibetan monks, or the sound of the ocean). Do yoga as part of foreplay, and enter her from the yabyum position in which the gentleman sits cross-legged, and the lady sits on his lap with her legs wrapped around his waist. For more about sacred or tantric sex, read books by Chogyam Trungpa Rinpoche or Margo Anand (see Recommended Reading).

Be a *Gentle*man

Cultivate her dreams, explore her fantasies, support her aspirations, help her to realize her desires, and her greatest desire will be to share it all with you.

Well, maybe not "all." Some of her deeper fantasies may always remain her secret. That's normal. In a Kinsey Institute study, 71 percent of men and 72 percent of women said they had fantasized while with partners to enhance sexual arousal, but 87 percent of the people who admitted having sex fantasies believed that their partners would respond unfavorably if they found out about them, so naturally, they never told.[7]

The best you can do to get your lady to open up completely is show and tell her that you're worthy of her trust, that you are a true *gentle*man, an adherent to the principles of these commandments, a knight of honor, courage, and compassion, on a continual quest for the Holy Grail that is her love and pleasure.

Recommended Reading

Anand, Margo. *The Art of Sexual Magic*. New York: Tarcher/Putnam, 1995.
Barbach, Lonnie, ed. *Pleasures*. New York: Doubleday, 1984.
————. *Erotic Interludes*. New York: Doubleday, 1986.
————. *The Erotic Edge*. New York: E. P. Dutton, 1994.
Bright, Susie, ed. *Herotica 2*. New York: Plume Press, 1992.
Califia, Pat. *Macho Sluts*. Boston: Alyson Publications, 1988.
————. *The Lesbian S/M Safety Manual*. San Francisco: Lace Publications, 1988.
————. *Sensuous Magic*. New York: Richard Kasak Books, 1992.
————. *Melting Point*. Boston: Alyson Publications, 1993.
————. *Doing It for Daddy*. Boston: Alyson Publications, 1994.
————. *Public Sex*. Pittsburgh: Cleis Press, 1994.
Estes, Clarissa Pinkola. *Women Who Run with the Wolves*. New York: Ballantine Books, 1992.
Friday, Nancy. *My Secret Garden*. New York: Simon & Schuster Pocket Books, 1973.
————. *Forbidden Flowers*. New York: Simon & Schuster Pocket Books, 1975.

[7]Reinisch, *Kinsey Institute New Report on Sex*, p. 92.

————. *Women on Top*. New York: Simon & Schuster Pocket Books, 1991.

Rednour, Shar, ed. *Virgin Territory*. New York: Richard Kasak Books, 1995.

Rice, Anne (writing as A. N. Roquelaure). *The Claiming of Sleeping Beauty*. New York: Plume, 1983.

Rinpoche, Chogyam Trungpa. *The Lion's Roar: An Introduction to Tantra*. Boston: Shambala Press, 1992.

Stevens, Serita. *Daughters of Desire*. New York: Leisure Books, 1987.

Tisdale, Sallie. *Talk Dirty to Me*. New York: Doubleday, 1994.

Ware, Ciji. *Island of the Swans*. New York: Bantam Books, 1989.

Dr. Susan Block's
10 Commandments *of a* Lady's Pleasure
(abbreviated version)

I Thou Shalt Pay Attention to the Details
of Her Desire

Learn to find and touch her personal "pleasure points." Like pressure
points that promote healing when touched, a lady's mental and physical
pleasure points are erotic entryways into her "armor" that allow her to receive pleasure.

2 Thou Shalt Stimulate Her Senses

Looking good is never bad. But most ladies are more auditory than
visual, so it's more vital that you *say* arousing things. It's also important
that you smell and taste nice. Take showers *before* going to bed instead
of *after* getting out. Eat lots of celery and cinnamon. Ladies are most sensitive to touch. Explore the sensual paradise of her body. Have "outercourse." Find her hottest spots. Pleasure her feet and give her *toegasms!*

3 Thou Shalt Compliment Her Meaningfully and
Often

Just because you've told her once doesn't mean you shouldn't tell her
again—and again. The type of compliment depends on the lady. Worship
her body, and she'll be more likely to want to share it with you. Respect
her mind, and she'll give you the key to unlock her desires . . .

4 Thou Shalt Encourage Her to Show and Tell You
How She Likes to Be Touched

Reassure her that it's okay for her to tell you what turns her on. Don't be
intimidated! Ask her to masturbate for you. Watch her carefully, not just
for your own excitement, but to see how she likes to be touched.

5 **THOU SHALT LISTEN TO HER . . .**
and learn about who she is, what she's been through, what she needs, and what she wants. If you listen, you'll discover the little girl inside your lady. Pleasure her, play with her, and she'll never grow old. Talk to her and, most of all, *listen* to her, and she'll never stop speaking to you.

6 **THOU SHALT MAKE HER LAUGH**
Laughter is a mental orgasm. Amuse your lady. Be a fool for love. Act like a bonobo chimpanzee. If you can make her laugh, you can win her heart, and her genitals will soon follow.

7 **THOU SHALT GIVE HER THINGS**
Since the dawn of humanity, when prehistoric gentlemen gave the best chunks of meat to the ladies they desired, men have successfully seduced women with gifts. The kind of gift depends on the lady and on you—it could be emerald earrings, sexy lingerie, a flower from a field, the gift of your emotional support, or creative talent. It's not that she doesn't "love you for yourself," it's just that a very primitive part of her responds to a gift as an erotic act.

8 **THOU SHALT EXUDE CONFIDENCE AND VULNERABILITY**
Your confidence makes her feel secure and excited at the same time. Your vulnerability makes you warmer and cuddlier, accessible, lovable. If you can combine confidence with vulnerability, you're probably the kind of person who can talk about your feelings. Good for you! Most modern ladies love that. The strong silent type is a sex symbol of the past, and a good thing, too, for he was often a secret psychopath.

9 **THOU SHALT HAVE FOREPLAY**
Foreplay is playful. Tease your lady's personal pleasure points wherever you find them. Be patient. Learn to lick, lap, and love it! Remember the key to female sexual pleasure: *Lubrication, lubrication, lubrication!*

1O **THOU SHALT FIND OUT WHAT HER DREAMS ARE
MADE OF . . .**
and help her to realize them, even if that just means talking to her about them. . . . Help her to explore, understand, and actualize her dreams, her hopes, her ambitions, her fantasies.

The

10

COMMANDMENTS

of a

GENTLEMAN'S

PLEASURE

I

THOU SHALT

Accept Him for Who He Is . . .

. . . not for what you wish he could be. Of course, every lady needs to be accepted for who she is, too, but this commandment is for the boys. A gentleman desperately needs to be accepted, appreciated, and approved of—especially by the lady in his life. The male of the species is particularly sensitive about being accepted because of his *castration anxiety*. He needs to know that you accept him as the male that he is, that you won't try to change him or cut off his balls.

The Heartbreak of Rejection

The opposite of acceptance is rejection. The male loathes rejection. The female does, too, of course. But the male is particularly sensitive because he tends to see rejection as an attack on his "manhood" (there go his balls again!). His desire to avoid rejection is so strong that if he just gets a whiff of it, he'll try to beat you to the punch and reject you first.

Male Perversity
Accepting him for who he is means: *Don't try to change him*. You may be able to change some little things about him—like getting him to

take a shower before going to bed, or having him caress your breasts without grabbing them, or making him take out the garbage before it starts to reproduce—but you can't change *who he is,* and he will resent the hell out of you for trying. Men are perverse that way.

This doesn't mean you should walk on eggshells around your guy. But if you're angry or upset about something, try to express your feelings without accusing or blaming him. In our society, the male is trained to respond defensively to anything perceived to be an attack (oh no, another assault on his family jewels!). If you put him on the defensive, he's no longer on your team.

Sexual Acceptance

The ultimate acceptance of the male is the act of sexual intercourse, when you accept him into your body. When a lady opens up her body to her primemate, wrapping him up in her warm, wet embrace, he feels like he has come home. When Max points to the V of my crotch and says, "That's where I live," I know he really means it.

Acceptance is to everyday life as surrender is to sexual fantasy. You can't fake it, you must feel it.

Gentlemen and Their Drives

Yes, women can be just as horny as men. But biological and social factors drive the male to have sex with more urgency than the female. This is partly because gentlemen have all that libido-driving testosterone, and because their penises are on the *outside* of their bodies, constantly reminding them to get laid *now.* Also, since society generally encourages men to pursue sex more than women, sex is more of a conscious, constant priority for most gentlemen than for most ladies.

Because the male tends to crave sex so much, he winds up feeling the loathsome sting of rejection fairly often. Each time your male primemate tries to embark upon sex and you reject him, he feels that awful pain. After a while, his male ego defense mechanism sets in. He can't bear the rejection, so he starts rejecting the female he perceives to be rejecting him (that's you!). He may find himself desiring other ladies he doesn't know well who haven't yet rejected him. Perhaps he'll get turned on by fantasy women, women in porn movies, women he doesn't care about, so he won't care if they accept or reject him. Or, stung so badly by rejection, he may lose interest in sex altogether. And neither of you will know why.

At this point, you will probably start missing sex. You may get very horny. If you do before his defenses have hardened him completely, you could save your sex life. But if you wait too long to invite and accept him into your body again, he could turn cold on you. He could well become the one pushing you away. He could even become your enemy.

This is not to say you should have sex when you don't want to. But do try to have it fairly regularly. Remember: "Use it or lose it" applies to your love life. When you're really not in the mood, at least say or do something sexually positive (e.g., hold him, tell him you love him and you think he's got a hot bod, kiss his penis, invite him to masturbate), so he doesn't feel totally rejected.

What If You Don't *Want* to Accept the Guy?

This might seem obvious, but it's an injunction so often ignored by otherwise intelligent women that it bears repeating:

If you simply can't accept the man in your life for who he is—or if he can't accept you for who you are—you shouldn't be with him!

That is, if "surrender" feels like you're being taken hostage in wartime, don't accept anything from the jerk. Don't allow abuse. If you're involved in an abusive relationship, get out and get help. Please!

I didn't create these commandments to help you to get along with an abusive asshole!

Even if he's not physically or verbally abusive, you may not want to accept him. The two of you may just not be a good match. Be honest with yourself as to who you are and what you need. Don't try to turn yourself into an emotional pretzel to fit his personality just because he's "eligible," and don't expect him to do that for you. Either accept him, or let him go.

We cannot choose our parents or children, but we can choose our primemates. And throughout nature, the female does most of the choosing. "Biologists now recognize that females across species exercise mate choice—that choice making is part of female nature . . . and may have played a very important part in the evolution of the species," according to science writer Mary Batten.[1]

Choice is crucial. Choose carefully *before* you get deeply involved. Never assume that "after the wedding" or "after the baby," he'll be different. He won't be, at least not in the way you expect.

If You Choose Him Wisely, You Can Accept Him Joyously

In our impersonal, fast-changing, cybernetic world, the male needs acceptance more than ever—sexual acceptance and emotional acceptance. Accepting him means not asking him to live up to your hidden expectations, but accepting him as you find him and rejoicing in all that he is.

Recommended Reading

Berkowitz, Bob. *What Men Won't Tell You but Women Need to Know.* New York: Avon Books, 1995.

Cabot, Tracy. *How to Make a Man Fall in Love with You.* New York: Dell, 1985.

Schlessinger, Laura. *Ten Stupid Things Women Do to Mess Up Their Lives.* New York: Random House, 1994.

Wallerstein, Judith S., and Sandra Blakeslee. *The Good Marriage.* Boston: Houghton Mifflin, 1995.

---

[1]Mary Batten, *Sexual Strategies: How Females Choose Their Mates* (New York: Putnam Publishing Group, 1992), p. 3.

2

THOU SHALT

Adore His Penis

Men love their own penises, and so should you. His penis is not just his greatest source of pleasure, it's his identity, his thrust into the future, his proudest possession, his best friend, his most powerful and most vulnerable body part. Adore it, adorn it, hold it, caress it, kiss it, lick it, suck it, praise it, play with it, tease it, torture it—*gently*, of course.[1] Talk to his penis (sometimes it may have more to say than he does!), develop a relationship with it, talk *about* it and how much you love it. Do this often. Several times daily is not too often.

Keep in mind that a man's penis is always outside his body, not hidden away like a woman's genitalia, so a guy tends to think about it a lot. He has to negotiate its position in his underwear, not to mention handle it every time he takes a whiz. When it gets hard, watch out! That thing moves and grows like Godzilla taking over downtown Tokyo! When it doesn't get hard, and it's "supposed" to get hard, it might as well be a flag flying at half-mast for a deeply beloved dead hero.

No matter how monogamous you are, you will always share your man with "someone" he loves at least as much as you: his dick.

---

[1]Unless he's a submissive masochist, in which case I suggest clothespins, rubber bands, or other convenient household implements of torture.

Try not to make him choose between you and his penis too often. That's just asking for trouble.

Touch His Penis

All men don't want the same things in life or in sex, but every man does want to have his penis touched. Men do like different types of touch; some like it soft and gentle, others rough and vigorous, some prefer the friction of dry touch, others want it wet and sensual. But all like *direct* touch.

When a gentleman's penis is stroked, all of him is stroked. It's his simplest, most basic pleasure. Touch it with your lips, your fingertips, your hands, your hair, your tongue, your tush, your nose, and your toes. Rub it between your breasts (that's *coitus a mammalia*). Rub your wet labia against it. Welcome it into you. Sit on it, spread for it, bend over for it. Hug and squeeze it while it's inside of you. Explore his other erogenous zones—the multiple pleasure points all over his body and in his mind. But you can never focus too much affectionate attention on a man's penis, even a sensitive man's.

Love it in sickness and in health, in hardness and in limpness.

Basically, the more harmoniously the three of you can live together, the happier all of you will be. . . .

The Order of Things

With gentlemen, it tends to be penis first. With ladies, it's vagina last. This may be the crux of the conflict we call the "Battle of the Sexes." The good news is that these apparently opposed approaches to sex can be quite compatible, as long as the male learns to arouse the female *before* penetrating her, and as long as the female learns to get to his dick as soon as possible. Yes, sometimes, you can even kiss his penis before you kiss his lips. I assure you, he won't mind.

If you *start* by paying lots of loving attention to his penis, then, when he's fully aroused, you can move on to his other body parts, intermittently returning to his main "member," and gradually you will eroticize his entire body. "Like a woman," he will become virtually orgasmic all over. Once his penis is hard, you can take a touch adventure all over his body (see Lady's Commandment #2: Thou Shalt Stimulate Her Senses, pages 11–22). Like a happy doggy with a hard-wagging "tail," he'll adore being petted and stroked all over.

Pet Peenie Names

Almost everyone with a beloved penis in their life has a pet name for it—peenie, weenie, peenie-weenie, peepee, peter, pickle, pecker, prick, rod, roger, dingaling, dork, dick, dong, schlong, schmuck, shaft, snake, salami, skin flute, hot dog, third leg, thunderbolt, cock, cocker-rocker, joint, johnson, tool, dipstick, joystick, jade stalk, machine, magic wand, member, meat, monster, manroot, manhood, middle leg, lovepump, lingam, vajra, wand of light, big stick, or little willie. Take your pick, or make up something special to suit your very special wonder worm.

Penis Games You Can Play

Desire the Penis
Reassure him that you love it, want it, and need it.

Admire the Penis
Talk about how good it feels, how beautiful it is, how hard it is, how big it is (unless that's obviously absurd). Talk about how much you love to suck it.

Baby the Penis
Talk babytalk to it, call it pet names, love it even when it's little and soft—and it won't stay little and soft very long!

Tease the Penis
. . . To make him slow down or last longer and enjoy it all the more.

"Fear" the Penis
Say, "Oh my, it's so big! How will I ever get that huge thing inside of me?"

Suck the Penis

Sucking, the essence of fellatio (from *fellare*, which, in Latin, means "to suck"), creates a vacuum, a negative pressure that actually draws blood into the penis, and that blood flow creates an erection. When a gentleman is aroused, blood gets pumped into his cock at six to eight times its normal rate. For sucking "to completion," see Gentleman's Commandment #10: Thou Shalt Swallow (pages 167–170).

Peenie Pop

Roll a small piece of ice around in your mouth until it melts, then suck him off. Use flavored ice and pretend it's a Popsicle!

Penis Bondage

Wrap it up in a silk stocking, a necktie, or a leather strap. The hornier he is, the tighter you can make it. You might even want to play Spank the Penis. Be careful, though—he's delicate down there!

Engulf the Penis

The greatest acceptance of a man is to accept his beloved penis into your beautiful body. Take a physically active role in intercourse. Remember, sexual intercourse is not just about the penis penetrating the vagina. It's also about the vagina engulfing the penis.

Quickie for His Dickie

Give your gentleman a nice quickie every so often. When he or you are in a hurry, but he wants sex for his penis's sake, and if you want sex too, or even if you don't want it, but you don't *mind* it, do it: Have a quickie. Even if you're not really into it. Just remind him that he owes you one—*your way.*

Penile Pleasure Points

The most sensitive part of the penis is the head or *glans*, especially the rim, including the *coronal ridge* and *frenulum*. Lick and suck the head right away, tonguing the tender rim, and he'll adore you instantly. This kind of love doesn't last forever, of course, but if you do it right, it's love at first lick. Then, again, if you're into playing the teasing game, don't even touch the head with your tongue until you can practically feel it throbbing for you. Then lightly embrace the head with your lips, feather-tickling the rim with your tongue tip.

Tease him like that, and he'll be wild. He'll do anything for you, take anything you dish out. This is a good time to tell him about one of your more bizarre sexual fantasies or ask him a favor or let him know you just dented his Harley—before engulfing him into bliss, the entrance to the top floor of the temple of the goddess, *your warm wet mouth*. If the ecstasy is just too intense, and he ejaculates into your mouth, don't panic (see Gentleman's Commandment #10: Thou Shalt Swallow, page 167). If he doesn't come, you've got some time to play. Open wide, let your lips go all the way down, twirl your tongue around, come up for air, and go at it again.

Which brings us to the *shaft* of the penis, also a major male pleasure point, though generally not quite as sensitive as the head and the rim. Most gentlemen can take a pretty hard squeezing of the shaft, as long as you don't bend, yank, or twist it! Talk to him about what kinds of strokes and licks he likes.

If your male primemate has a foreskin,[2] you can play with it, even when he doesn't have an erection. Lick the sensitive upper edge of the foreskin. You can even stick your tongue inside it and tickle the head of his cock with the tip of your tongue. Stroke and pull it up and down as his penis gets harder and harder, pushing your tongue out. A great Penis Pleasure Game for the uncut gentleman. Make sure he keeps his foreskin clean, of course—you don't want to be licking up lint!

Testicles and Tushyholes

If the penis is the romantic lead of the male sex show, the *testicles* are the supporting character actors. The testicles—or "balls," "nuts," "cojones," "family jewels"—are his factories of future generations,

---

[2]Max calls it a *cappuccino*. Yes, the same Renaissance Italian monks who made the coffee also wore hoods that resembled foreskins.

the hormone generators. Within them lies the source of maleness, *testosterone*. In Old Testament times, taking an oath was very serious business, and to indicate your sincerity, you put your hand on the testicles of the man to whom you were swearing. That's right, you touched his balls! Think about that next time you swear on a Bible or sign a contract. Supposedly, this meant if you broke your oath, his progeny could come get you. From this incredible act of testicle-handling, we get terms like *testament* and *testify*. You can testify to your love by handling his testicles, stroking them, spanking them lightly, licking them, kissing them, sucking them into your mouth, gently pulling on the *scrotum* (the skin surrounding the testicles), gently but firmly pushing them up toward his penis, maybe even tying them up.

Another nearby pleasure point is the *perineum*, which is halfway between the base of the testicles (i.e., the scrotal sac) and the anus. Stroke, press, and lick this very sensitive area to give him delicious twinges of pleasure.

Which brings us to his *anus* (also called backdoor, butthole, asshole, and my personal favorite, tushyhole), a major pleasure point for some gentlemen and a point of high anxiety for others.

Many pleasure points are also points of pain, fear, disgust, and embarrassment, and the butthole is a classic.

If it's a point of problem feelings for you, you may find just reading this paragraph to be difficult. So, take a deep breath and relax. *Skip this section if you're not relaxed.* Nature lined the human anus with a wealth of nerve endings so we would all feel good about going to the bathroom (way back before there were bathrooms). These nerve endings can respond with intense pleasure (or pain) to any form of stimulation, not just to "elimination." That's why some people, male and female, love to have their buttholes played with—caressed, tickled, licked, tongued, penetrated. Likewise, some people like to do the licking, caressing, and penetrating. For them, anal sex is a pleasure point. Of course, for some people, male and female, just the idea of licking the anus is like sticking your tongue into a sewer. If you're one of those people, far be it from me to try to persuade you to try it. You either have a "taste" for anal, or you don't, though it's possible to develop one.

But Wait—The Anus as a Male *Pleasure Point?*

Women's anuses can be just as sensitive (or uptight) as men's. But the anus is the *only* part of the male genital area that can be pene-trated (except for his peehole, but *don't* try penetrating that unless you really know what you're doing). Also, in a way, just as a lady has a G spot, a gentleman has a "P spot," the very sensitive area of his *prostate* that you can reach with your finger, butt plug, strap-on, or whatever you're using (please, darling, nothing breakable). Press his P spot and he'll go mad with excitement. And please understand:

Just because a man enjoys having his anus licked or penetrated does NOT "mean" that he is gay.

Sure, gay men have a lot of anal sex. That's mainly because they don't have any other orifices to choose from in that area. But feeling plea-sure from receiving anal sex has nothing to do with sexual orientation. Many heterosexual ladies like it, and many heterosexual gentlemen like it. The anus is a powerful pleasure point, plain and simple.

Well, maybe not *so* simple. Most of us have rather complex, love-hate, mixed-up feelings about our precious, uptight assholes. If you're new to anal, go very slowly, millimeter by millimeter. Since the anus doesn't self-lubricate as the vagina does, you must make sure it is clean and wet. You may wish to start with your tongue. If you're too squeamish to lick, or if you're at all unsure about the health of your partner, use a lubricant. Make sure it's water-based if you're using condoms, which you should be if you're not absolutely monogamous. If you are not strictly monogamous and you are into anal, you must make latex your friend. Whatever you do, be careful not to ram any-thing hard into the anus, or you will tear the tender flesh. Keep in mind that the AIDS virus and others are said to spread most easily through rough, unprotected anal sex.

Nipples

A man's nipples are, technically, not part of his genitalia, but they can be very sensitive, with a hot line to his penis. If you can just get him to relax enough, you can suck and squeeze his nipples into ec-stasy. Again, having pleasure points in the nipples has nothing to do with sexual orientation.

Penis Problems

Back to the penis. The human penis is a marvelous, but rather moody appendage. Plato wrote, "In man, the nature of the genital organs is disobedient and self-willed, like a creature deaf to reason, all because of its frenzied lusts."[3] But your penis, or your primemate's penis (if you're the one driving the vulva), can be your friend— *maybe your best friend.* That's why you may well have a pet name for it, and that's why you should celebrate with it in times of joy, and help it out in times of distress.

> *His penis, his rod, and his staff, they comfort him, give pleasure, relief, and express his deepest passions.*

Unfortunately, his penis also expresses some of his deepest *fears.* This can result in penis problems like premature ejaculation or temporary impotency or the desire for extreme pain. That's why it's important to learn about the penis, whether you have one or not.

It is beyond the scope of these commandments to deal thoroughly with the "penis problems" listed below. If your male primemate has any of these problems, you might want to take a look at one of the books under Recommended Reading and/or consult a sex therapist or sex-friendly urologist.

Sexual Quick Draw Syndrome
Nature favors premature ejaculators, guys that shoot their wad into the next generation almost before they know it. Evolution has favored those males who could come as fast as possible, that is, before predators—ancient saber-toothed cats or modern-day parents—arrived to ruin the mood.

> *But just because premature ejaculation is natural doesn't mean it's desirable.*

Gentlemen must be educated in ejaculation control. How else will they learn? After all, someone had to toilet-train them, right? But

---

[3] Quoted in Kenneth Purvis, *The Male Sexual Machine: An Owner's Manual* (New York: St. Martin's Press, 1992), p. 64.

nobody is ejaculation-trained! Well, there are whole books about it, but here are a few basic tips on how to deal with your male prime-mate's sexual quick draw syndrome:

1. Premature ejaculation is extremely common among young men. If your male primemate is under twenty-five, and he's quick on the trigger, he'll probably slow down as he gets older. In the meantime, after he comes, just wait the few minutes it takes for him to get another erection, and do it again when he's ready. If he ejaculates prematurely the first time, the next time he will last longer simply because he has less fluid in his seminal vesicles[4] and less urgency to release it.

2. Ejaculating before you want to—whether it's after ten minutes or ten seconds—can be considered a "weakness." That means you need to "work out" the right muscles. If the muscles in your thighs are weak and you want to run longer, you work out your thigh muscles. So what muscle should a gentleman exercise to strengthen his ability to maintain an erection in different sexual positions without ejaculating? (Contrary to popular belief, the penis itself is *not* a muscle—nor does it have a bone, even though they call erections "boners"). Answer: His PC muscle. No, it's not his politically correct muscle or his personal computer muscle; it's the *pubococcygeus* (PC) muscle group that runs from the pubic bone in front to the tailbone in back and supports the pelvic floor. This is the muscle that spasms during orgasm in the male *and* the female.

    To find your PC muscle, pretend that you're urinating and want to stop the flow of urine by squeezing an internal muscle. Feel that? That's your PC muscle. Flex it for a couple of seconds, then release. Try not to hold your breath while flexing. Now, get your male primemate to do this exercise—just squeezing and releasing—ten times in the morning and ten times in the evening, gradually holding it longer each time, and he will eventually gain strength and control. Actually, it's an amazing exercise. You can do it anytime, anywhere—sitting, standing,

---

[4]The *seminal vesicles* are a couple of little storage pouches behind the prostate where sperm is mixed with the rest of the seminal fluid before it's shot through the shaft and into the world.

walking around, or lying down—and no one will see what you're doing. Ten times in the morning, ten times in the evening. You should do it regularly, too. A strong PC muscle enhances female orgasm tremendously.

3. Try the Stop/Start Technique. Just like the name says, this method involves arousing the penis to the point *before* the point of no return and then stopping, pulling out if necessary, and letting his erection go down a bit before resuming the stroking, sucking, or thrusting. The stop/start exercise trains your gentleman's big head and little head to "recognize" the points or stages of pleasure *before* the point of no return. Then it trains him to stop—maybe for half a second, maybe for about a minute—so he doesn't come. It's a simple exercise that sex therapists and surrogates have been teaching for years, and it really works after about a month or two of practice, *if* you practice.

4. Try the Squeeze Technique. This is the same as the Stop/Start Technique, but just as he stops, you or he squeezes the rim of the penis, between the head and the shaft, holding the thumb on top and the first and second fingers underneath. That's the most popular "spot" for the Squeeze Technique, but there's another spot right in the middle of the base of the penis, above the scrotum, where it meets the pubic bone. Max and some other guys I've talked to swear this is a surefire come-stopper.

5. A little alcohol can help some gentlemen with sexual quick draw syndrome last longer. But be careful: it renders some guys limp as a celery stick in a day-old Bloody Mary. As the Porter says to Macduff in Shakespeare's *Macbeth*, "it provokes the desire, but it takes away the performance."

6. Every guy comes too fast *sometimes* due to stress, novelty, performance anxiety, or excitement. If your male primemate just does it occasionally, please don't make a big deal about it. You're likely to make it worse. Just gently and playfully start going through some of the above activities. They're great sexual muscle-building exercises, even if you don't have "penis problems." And don't let the fact that he came before you stop you from coming. As a matter of fact, if you (cheerfully) start to masturbate or request that he eat you out or screw you with a

dildo (remember, always keep a "backup system" for his "hard drive"), he'll probably get another hard-on.

7. If your guy is over thirty, chronically trigger-happy, and has "no luck" with the above exercises, he probably has some internal sexual conflicts that he needs to work out to be able to relax and relate sexually, as well as control himself. As Dr. Dudley Danoff, urologist to the stars, who claims to have seen more than 100,000 different peckers in his professional life, says: "Your penis doesn't have a mind of its own; it reads your mind . . . the behavior of the penis is a more accurate barometer of who you are at any particular moment than your own conscious assessment."[5]

So, what is his quick-to-come, quick-to-go prick telling you? Could it be that he subconsciously wants to get sex over with? If you're brave, discuss this with him—but it can get you into pretty tough territory, perhaps regarding his hostility toward women, his fears of abandonment (so he comes quick and abandons first), his guilt about sex, his conflicts over pleasure. Perhaps he could benefit from talking with a sex therapist. You may want to contact one together.

8. Keep in mind that coming "too fast" is relative. If your problem is simply that he comes before you, then just make sure that he gives you an orgasm or two before he gets into any of your orifices or, if he's lightning-fast, before you touch his penis at all. Tell him to study Lady's Commandments 1 to 10 for that, with a special emphasis on #9: Thou Shalt Have Foreplay (page 59).

Penis Size

Most men have what I call a "Howard Sperm Complex": They think their penis is too small.[6] As the saying goes, "Women don't have penis envy, men do." For the most part, guys are the ones worrying about how their penis measures up sizewise with other guys. It's the oldest male sex hang-up in the book. Which is too bad. Too many men waste valuable sexual energy thinking about how big or small

---

[5]Dudley Danoff, *Superpotency* (New York: Warner Books, 1993), pp. 21–22.
[6]Based on "shock jock" radio personality Howard Stern, who claims to have a minuscule penis.

their tool is instead of thinking about how to use it to give themselves and their lovers pleasure.

"It Ain't the Meat; It's the Motion"

It's not just in the penis, it's in the pelvis. That's what I think, but
then, I'm a woman. Most surveys give no indication that penis size
is very important to most women. The human vagina displays
an amazing ability to shrink and expand to accommodate all penis
sizes and thus to provide similar degrees of friction. In fact, bigger-
than-average cocks are often painful to women, especially if the
guy is so enthralled with the dimensions of his endowment that he
doesn't bother to learn how to use it sensitively. Most ladies agree
that it's no good being built like a bull if all you can do is charge like
one.

But try telling this to most men; they don't believe you! There's a
great scene in Philip Kaufman's movie *Henry and June*, based on
the diaries of Anaïs Nin. Anaïs is having a mad, passionate affair
with Henry Miller, they've just made love, and Anaïs is telling
Henry what a wonderful lover he is, how he's so much better than
her husband, Hugo, who's very awkward and unsatisfying sexually,
how she prefers making love to Henry for many reasons, one of
which is that Henry's penis is *smaller* than Hugo's. It's a great moment because you can see that Anaïs is sincere in her enthusiasm for
Henry's smaller penis, but Henry looks extremely upset about this
"compliment."

There are exceptions, of course, but basically, most gentlemen are
far more into "big dick worship" than most ladies are. Porno stars like
Long Dong Silver, who *supposedly* has an eighteen-inch "dong" that
can be tied in a knot, are male sex heroes. Very few ladies are interested in a date with a Long Dong Silver–type. *Why* do men admire
and even desire such ridiculously big dicks? Perhaps it is an unconscious sadistic wish to impale the female; maybe because a lot of men
think of sex as a sport, and they think of a big penis as a strong pitch-
ing arm or a great golf swing.

But why so much penis-size *anxiety?* Why so many Howard Sperm
Complexes? A few reasons:

1. Boys see their fathers' penises at an early age and worry that they won't "catch up." Most Dads don't explain that they will. It might help if they did.

2. Glances at other men in locker rooms are made end-on. The other guy's penis seems larger because a man sees his own from above, a perspective that makes a penis seem smaller because of foreshortening.

3. Flaccid penises vary dramatically in size, but erect they vary far less. Gentlemen with penises that are small when flaccid can develop tremendous complexes even though their penises might be average (five–seven inches) or even bigger than average when erect.

4. Too many porno movies! All the guys in porno movies have *huge* hot dogs. If your man's understanding of other men's penises comes primarily from porno movies, it's not surprising he has a size complex. Since images of erect penises are virtually banned everywhere but in hard-core pornography, where all the dicks are much larger than average, many men in our society get their vision of a "proper penis" from porno movies.

5. Men are kept ignorant by a general male reluctance to openly discuss intimate sexual matters with each other, except in terms of bragging; so the myth persists that penis size is of tremendous importance to ladies. It's important to *some* ladies: size queens with a deep dish who feel the need for a giant johnson. But not most ladies. To most ladies, the most important aspect of a penis is not how big it is, but how hard it is . . . which brings us to . . .

Impotency

When the flag flies at half-mast, the people mourn. Which is exactly what you shouldn't do! Here are some things you should do:

1. Continue having sex. Why should sex stop just because the penis isn't erect? John, one of my therapy clients, twenty-seven years old, had been impotent for a year. He'd been to a urologist, so he knew it wasn't a physical problem. He and his

twenty-five-year-old wife, Sara, had "tried everything," but he just couldn't get it up. I could hear his anguish, and my heart went out to this young man who only wanted to make love to his wife. But I could also hear how narrow he was in his approach to sex. Basically, he felt he couldn't have any kind of sex without an erection. He did say that he felt excited sometimes, just no hard-on. "In fact," he said, "I'm getting kind of excited now just talking about this."

"Why don't you make love to Sara, then?" I suggested.

He said something to the effect of "Huh? How?"

Since Sara was there and eager to help, I asked her to lie back, close her eyes, and masturbate as I whispered a bit of erotic encouragement. John watched her touch herself. "God, she's sexy," he sighed, "I wish I could get a hard-on so I could make love to her. Jesus, this is frustrating!"

"John," I said, "stop thinking about your erection. Think about Sara. Make love to her. Use your mouth, your hands, your chest, your arms, your legs, your voice, use a vibrator, *use your head*—use whatever you've got."

After a bit of the old hem-and-haw, John did just that, Sara proceeded to have a highly audible orgasm, and lo and behold, John had himself a hammer-hard erection, and they were still going at it when I left them alone. Moral of story: You do not need an erection to share many erotic pleasures. And the sheer act of sharing these pleasures with abandon, virtually forgetting about his penis, can make it hard.

2. Max's home remedy is cayenne pepper. He eats it with everything but ice cream. We call it "Peenie Power Powder." He says it thins the blood and keeps the dick hard. Sure keeps his hard all the time.

3. The PC muscle exercise I gave you for help with premature ejaculation problems also helps give your guy firmer, more long-lasting erections. So, altogether now: Squeeze . . . release . . . squeeze . . . release . . .

4. If he's over forty or so, you just might have to work a little harder to get him hard. This is a fact of the male aging process, though it does vary from gentleman to gentleman. Your best bet is lots of oral sex. That vacuum-sucking effect works won-

ders. Also, morning sex, when male potency tends to peak, often proves more successful in terms of erections than evening sex.

5. The Victorians used to think that overuse of the penis led to impotency, but modern science has revealed the opposite is true. *Underuse* is more likely to lead to early impotency. If you two have not done it in five years, don't be surprised if he can't do it at all. *"Use it or lose it"* is a penis credo.

6. Impotency can be a purely physical problem because of disease, such as diabetes, injury, or drug use, either medicinal or recreational. Your gentleman should, of course, consult with the appropriate doctor about the best remedies for this. Keep in mind that orgasm may still be possible for him, even if erection is not. If you love and care for him, don't stop having sex just because he doesn't get erections, and don't stop following this commandment.

What If *You* Have a Problem with *His* Penis?

If he's hurting you with his penis, if he's using it like a pile driver and you don't *like* him using it like a pile driver, you must let him know, and figure out a way that he can do his thing without hurting you. The commandment is to "adore his penis," not to suffer for it.

Is His Penis a Pest?
Does it seem to be forever nudging you for sex like a hungry child? What if you're not in the mood? Don't have sex if you really don't want to, but be certain to reassure him verbally and physically so he doesn't take it as a personal rejection. Also, support his need to masturbate, with and without you, so that his penis never feels deprived of sexual release when you're out of town or not in the mood.

Enjoy the Show
Sometime when you're not in the mood for penetration, but you are in the mood for love, you might ask him to masturbate right in front of you. Most women are put off by the idea of a man masturbating for them, *until* they actually experience it! Then, they are almost always

amazed by how erotic it is. If you've never tried it, request that your primemate stand up and stroke his sexy shaft as you sit back and enjoy the show. You may discover, as I have, that your masturbating man, penis in hand, is a glorious sight to behold.

Recommended Reading

Danoff, Dudley Seth. *Superpotency*. New York: Warner Books, 1993.

Morin, Jack. *Anal Pleasure and Health*. Burlingame, CA: Down There Press, 1986.

Paglia, Camille. *Sexual Personae*. New York: Vintage Books, 1990.

———. *Vamps and Tramps*. New York: Vintage Books, 1994.

Purvis, Kenneth. *The Male Sexual Machine: An Owner's Manual*. New York: St. Martin's Press, 1992.

3

THOU SHALT

Be a Source of Beauty in His Life

. . . whether it's in the way you look, walk, dress, dance, or smile. Most gentlemen, unless they're legally blind, are very visual. They like to touch, smell, taste, and listen to you, but they love to look at you. *What* they love you to look like varies according to the particular man, but there's no getting around the importance of appearances even to the most sensitive and feminist of gentlemen.

Looks aren't "everything," but they're a big thing. Most men are at least part-voyeur; they like to look—some to the point that their bulging eyes and open jaws resemble those of a rabid dog. That's why they're generally better map readers than women, and your body is a map of their desire.

The modern female commonly considers the male to be shallow if he is attracted primarily to what is merely "skin deep." Try to understand that your guy may very well want to get to know you, but the place he starts his "research" is your body.

The Male Looks for "Prey"
In prehistoric times, men hunted both for food and mates, and they got very involved with *looking* for prey, developing their sense of sight as a vital part of their sexuality. We may have come a long way from our cave days, but men still hunt for what looks good

to them. Because a gentleman is turned on or off by how you look doesn't mean he's sexist; it's just that he's been trained by Mother Nature.

Accent Your Assets

You don't have to be model-perfect to be a source of beauty in a man's life. You can be fat, flat, cross-eyed, or crippled. Just find out which parts of your body he *does* like and accentuate their beauty. If you don't know what he likes, accentuate the parts of yourself that *you* like. Discreetly cover up what you don't like (as long as it's not your whole body!), and wear things to draw attention to the parts of your body that you feel good about. Show them off for him.

Be a pleasure to his eyes, and he'll never take them off you. . . .

Don't be squeamish, now. Remember the wise words of that vintage-raunchy sex goddess Mae West, "It's better to be looked over than to be overlooked."[1]

Dress for Sex—At Least Sometimes

Wear lingerie. Lingerie feels cool and looks hot. It teases as it pleases, reveals as it conceals. Many gentlemen find it more exciting than total nudity. Ever since the invention of the corset (or before), gentlemen have been fascinated and even obsessed with what goes on underneath it all.

What does your primemate respond to—the sensual elegance of silk? the old-fashioned romanticism of antique lace? the innocence of pure white cotton? the wild animal excitement of leather? the high-tech kinkiness of latex, rubber, and PVC? the unapologetic lustiness of black or red anything?

Whatever he likes, why not wear it tonight?

---

[1]From the 1934 film *Belle of the Nineties*, which Mae West scripted as well as starred in.

Wearing lingerie, or some kind of "sex clothing," implies that you're preparing for sex; you're thinking about sex while getting dressed. Men who love sex love a woman who thinks about it, dresses up for it.

Of course, less sexually secure guys can be literally frightened by blatantly sexual undergarments. I remember the third night I slept with an ex-boyfriend I'll call Waldo. I wanted to wear something sexy, so I put on a violet lace corset, black stockings, and high heels. I looked myself over in the mirror and felt luminously sexual. "Uhhh . . . What are you supposed to be?" Waldo asked, abruptly transforming my erotic excitement into awful, abject embarrassment. Turned out Waldo preferred cotton leotards and kneesocks. Turned out *I* preferred not to be with Waldo. A man who doesn't appreciate a lady's efforts to dress up in sexy lingerie is *not* the man for that lady . . .

Wear His Clothes
The male often gets aroused by seeing his female primemate in his "male" clothing—his boxer shorts, undershirts, T-shirts, hats, ties, whatever fits you or just looks hot on you. Try it; it will make him want to be all over you just like his clothes are. Try wearing one of his dress shirts with your garter belt and stockings underneath.

Thou Shalt Show Off!
If you can't deal with public exhibitionism, at least try it in private. Put on a strip show for him. Dress provocatively, then tease, flash, turn away before exposing yourself, unbutton or unsnap slowly, play with yourself, bend over, dance enticingly, shimmy up to him. Practice in front of the mirror. Or just do it for him spontaneously. Try doing mini-stripteases when you're undressing for bed. If you're not in the mood for serious lingerie, a little sensuous strip before bed can be just as enticing. Flash him as you get dressed in the morning. Throughout the day, show him a nipple here, an ass cheek there, glimpses of your naked beauty. If stripping isn't your speed, learn to belly-dance. Or at least, do a nice little square-dance in your knickers, darling.

Surprise him with visual treats. Let him "catch" you masturbating or dirty dancing when he least expects it. Let him see you naked, unmasked. You really have nothing to hide, you know.

Artificial Beauty

Nature can be beautiful, but there's nothing wrong with improving on nature and enhancing your looks both to attract males and to impress other females, including yourself. Putting together your hair, makeup, outfit, and accessories is an art more ancient than Cleopatra. There is nothing weak or unfeminist about it. Well-applied makeup actually tends to increase your power. I know, many men *say* they don't like makeup. All I can say is that sometimes I wear makeup, sometimes I don't. When I do, every male around me—from my husband to my employees to my banker to the maitre d' at my local restaurant—is much more likely to do my bidding, with a smile on his face.

One reason some men tell you they don't like makeup is that they're afraid you'll attract other men.

Body Modification

Body modification is anything permanent: tattoos, piercings, silicon, plastic surgery. Don't modify your body just for a man (though you may agree on something like a tattoo for you); *do it for yourself*. You're the one who always has to live with it. Don't tattoo his name anywhere on your body unless he does the same with yours, and your relationship is as permanent as that ink.

Being Cute

Beauty is not all about being drop dead gorgeous. Beauty is also about being cute. In most cases, cuteness is easier to achieve than gorgeousness, and in its own way, it can be just as sexy. Even your flannel nightgown or big cotton T-shirt can be sexy in a cute and cuddly sort of way.

Let Him Watch You Go Down on Him

Gentlemen like oral sex partly because it feels so good and partly because it *looks* so good. Ladies generally close their eyes when receiving oral sex, but not guys—are you kidding? They don't want to miss anything!

*Most men love to watch, and they like nothing better than to watch
their beloved member go in and out of their lover's lovely mouth.*

When receiving oral, most men will maneuver themselves into
the prime position for watching. At the high point, some men love
to ejaculate all over a woman's face or in her hair or on her breasts,
though most women find this particular aspect of oral sex (getting
semen in your eyes or your ears or up your nose) to be rather rude and
even disgusting. I admit it's not one of my personal favorites. But I
also know it's not necessarily true that these men want to demean
women. Sometimes, they just like to *see* their beautiful delicious
semen all over their beautiful delicious lover. To them, it's a work of
art. Not that that's going to make you feel better about getting a glob
of hot sperm in your eye, ladies, but there it is. At least you know he's
not really trying to demean you. It is possible that the same man can
be both a sensitive feminist and enjoy squirting all over your face.
He's just very *visual*.

Here's Looking at You
Visual arousal is also why some gentlemen like to *give* oral sex to
a lady: They get a good up-close look at that vulva! Many women
are shy about "showing" their vulva, even to their lovers. That's
one reason some men go to strip clubs, to *see* that elusive vulva that
their wives won't show them. So, don't be shy now. Show your
primemate he's got everything he needs right in front of his sticky
wet face.

Enjoy Your Body

The more you enjoy your own body, the more he will. No gentleman
is ever turned on when a lady says, "I hate my body." He may try to
reassure you, but inside he's feeling queasy. I don't care who your man
is, your self-loathing is his biggest turn-off, even if he seems to pro-
voke it.

*Whatever you do, do not put your sex life on hold until you lose
ten pounds or because you hate your breasts, your cellulite, or
your wrinkles.*

Not that it's easy to have a healthy attitude about the female body, what with the media presenting us with an "ideal" female body (tiny waist, small buns, lean legs, slim arms, and *big knockers*) that is actually a freak of nature, only achievable with the help of plastic surgery.

I didn't say it was easy to love your body in all its sexy imperfections. But just because it isn't easy doesn't mean it isn't important to your man's pleasure, not to mention your well-being. Consider it a meditation. Accept your own flesh, your own limits, your own loveliness.

> *Loving your body, relaxing, accepting, and enjoying it even as you continue to do sexy little things to enhance it, is the greatest beauty treatment of all.*

Recommended Reading

Brown, Helen Gurley. *Having It All*. New York: Simon & Schuster, 1982.

Chopra, Deepak. *Ageless Body, Timeless Mind*. New York: Harmony Books, 1993.

Keefe, Tim. *Some of My Best Friends Are Naked: Interviews with Seven Erotic Dancers*. San Francisco: Barbary Coast, 1993.

Sprinkle, Annie. *Post Porn Modernist*. Amsterdam: Torch Books, 1991.

Williamson, Marianne. *A Woman's Worth*. New York: Random House, 1993.

4

THOU SHALT

Inspire Him

The Thirst for Inspiration

One of every man's greatest pleasures is to feel inspired. Within every
gentleman is an artist of sorts, an "inner" poet or philosopher, or
maybe just a dreamer, thirsting for inspiration from you, his primemate, his muse. When you inspire him, you ignite his passion, you set
his soul on fire, you enlighten him, you direct him to the right path,
you give him hope and a reason to work his tail off.

Your intelligence, spirituality, beauty, and integrity are great inspirations to your man, and I'll get more deeply into those by the end of
this commandment. But your pleasure is his greatest, and your sexual
pleasure is his sweetest inspiration. As Max often reminds me: *Men
work to get laid*—either by one special person or by everybody they
meet, or something in between. Inspire him to work, to live, to love,
to please you. Inspire him to make you come and come and come to
him.

Most men love sex (and the few who don't are lying!). And
most gentlemen love ladies who love sex. Your sexual pleasure ful-
fills your man and puts him in touch with profound emotions
which he otherwise represses, making him feel more potent and
more sensitive at the same time. Your pleasure can be his greatest

therapy. It can be an answer to his fervent prayer. It can actually heal his pain.

Shine a light upon his path to your pleasure points.
Show him the way to your Holy Grail.

Open yourself up to him, body and soul. Try to be fully "present" when you engage in sex. The ancient Roman poet Ovid spoke for most gentlemen when he wrote in *The Art of Love,* "I hate a woman who offers herself because she ought to do so, and, cold and dry, thinks of her sewing when she's making love." If you're thinking of your "sewing," or your morning office meeting, or what the kids are up to, or picking up the dry cleaning, you will not inspire your man.

A Gentleman Loves Pleasing a Lady

That's because he is inspired by pleasing you, by getting you to *respond* to him. The more he adores you, the more your pleasure becomes his pleasure. But he doesn't always know *how* to please you. So, you may have to ask for and even instruct your man in what pleases you (if you're shy about telling him, suggest he check out this book). He may resist being instructed. Remember, most men are perverse that way. He may think it means you don't "accept him." Reassure him that you do accept him, but don't give up the instruction.

To give him the pleasure of your inspiration, you must teach him to give *you* pleasure, but you have to instruct him in a way that he's receptive to learning. This can get tricky. Don't blame and accuse him for "just not getting it." Translate your pleasure into a language he understands.

Your Orgasms Are His Reward

Dan and Nancy (married fourteen years, with two kids and an active membership in the local church) called me for advice about improving their waning sex life. First I spoke to Dan. He informed me that his deepest erotic yearning was to be sexually dominated by his wife. He desperately wanted Nancy to wear the leather dominatrix outfit he'd bought her, which had just hung in the back of the closet since the day he brought it home. Then he wanted her to tie him up with silk scarves, spank him, tease him, torture him, and force him to have sex with her. He described *his* desires to me in great detail. But when I asked what he thought Nancy wanted out of sex, he paused, then confessed that he had no idea what Nancy wanted since she never talked about sex, certainly not during sex. She was "passive," he said, and that was the crux of what was driving him crazy. He explained that since he was always the leader—at work, at home, in bed—he wanted her to take charge for a change. He seemed to feel that it would inspire him.

It sounded somewhat kinky but reasonable, so when I spoke to Nancy shortly afterwards, I asked her what she thought of Dan's desire for her to dominate him. "Oh, that's what he always wants," she sighed wearily. She also said that no, she never wore the dominatrix outfit because it made her feel "silly," and since he didn't force the issue, it stayed in the closet.

"What do *you* want out of sex with Dan?" I asked her.

"Tenderness," she replied after a reflective pause. "Warmth. Love. I want him to make love to me tenderly, and he hardly ever really does that anymore."

As a sex therapist who works with a lot of men, I could understand Dan's desire, and as a woman who has a lot of sex, I could understand Nancy's. I asked Nancy to try to get over her feelings of "silliness" and put on the leather dominatrix garb just for that night. I told her to take a deep breath, close her eyes, and visualize herself as being infinitely strong and irresistibly sexy. Then I told her to order Dan to lie on their bed, tie him up securely, spank him a little, get him good and aroused, and then tell him exactly what *she* wanted him to do, how she needed for him to make love to her with the tenderness she deserved. If he protested that this wasn't the kind of domination he had in mind, she should remind him that *she's* the boss and he's all tied up, so he'd better listen up and follow her orders.

She agreed to implement my "plan," and they both called back the next day and told me about their incredible night. First she dominated him just like he'd always fantasized, then he made love to her more lovingly than he had in years.

> *Most men want to give women what they need and desire,*
> *especially sexually.*

You just have to instruct your man in a way he can understand (you may have to tie him up!). Your orgasms are his reward; they inspire him. He'll love doing whatever it is that makes you come for him.

Let Him Know You've Come

Since ladies tend not to ejaculate during orgasm, there's no tangible evidence that they've come. This is incredibly frustrating for the male. Some men desire sex with other men just because of the joy of seeing that shooting semen, and knowing for sure that there's been a climax.

Female orgasm is much more mysterious than male. My male callers and clients are constantly asking me, "How do I know when she's come? Is it when she starts breathing really heavy? Is it when her breasts flush? Is it when she gets really wet inside?" All of these symptoms are signs of female excitement, but not necessarily orgasm. I used to think it was only the really insensitive guys who had no idea when their own wives or girlfriends had orgasms, but then I found myself hearing the same complaint from men I considered sensitive as well as from lesbian women: "I don't know whether she's coming or not . . . I think she is . . . I hope she is . . . Do *you* think she is?"

The bottom line is that the human female is tough to read orgasmically. To someone who desperately wants to please her, who craves the inspiration of her orgasmic response, this can be confusing and unsettling. So, if you really want to give your gentleman plea-sure, let him know when you come. Send him the message, the Good News, the Lord hath come and *the Lady is coming . . .*

You can let him know, in part, through your body language. But body language is tough to control when you're coming. Besides, you're usually doing it in the dark, so how's he going to see your breasts flush? Let him know through *vocal* language, even if all you say is "ohhhhh yes!" (or "oh no!"). He loves to hear your feedback.

> *Your orgasmic outcry is an exquisite inspiration,*
> *and a marvelous catalyst to simultaneous orgasm.*

Vocalizing tends to enhance your pleasure as well, providing an audio dimension to your release of tension. It feels great to scream with pleasure, to call his name (no mistakes, now!). When you call out to him, you share your pleasure with him. And shared pleasure, like a shared meal or a shared sunset, is so much better than one enjoyed alone.

What If You Don't Know If You've Come?

Some of my female sex therapy clients tell me that they *don't know* whether or not they've had an orgasm. Nine times out of a ten, after a bit of discussion, we both realize that they haven't, in fact, climaxed. Sometimes they say they "don't know" because they're just too embarrassed to admit they've never come (especially if they're seeing me with their male primemates), though often they genuinely don't know due to a lack of basic education about their own sexuality. Once they learn to do what it takes for them to come to a climax, they definitely *know* it because they most definitely *feel* it.

Breathe into Orgasm

If orgasms don't come easily for you, don't wait for your primemate to press the right button, and don't fake it, either! Instead of "thinking of your sewing," focus on your breathing. Learn to breathe into your orgasmic state. The vital vapor of life—and sex—is breath. But all too often, during life—and sex—we forget to breathe.

> *We hold our breath in fear and out of excitement, effectively cutting ourselves off from our most basic source of power.*

Open yourself up to the power and pleasure of your breath. Inhale deeply and slowly, and exhale even more slowly. Imagine that you are breathing *into* your vulva and vagina, as you squeeze and release your PC muscles (the same muscles you squeeze when you want to stop yourself from urinating). With each deep breath, you might also imagine ocean waves crashing against the "shore" between your legs, each wave bigger than the one before, until you are finally overwhelmed by a tidal wave of liberating pleasure. Or you could let more obviously erotic images—sexy people doing sexy things with you or *to* you—flicker across the screen in the Theater of Your Mind.

Basically, no matter how "inorgasmic" you think you are, if you breathe deeply and slowly "into" your pelvis, if you let yourself relax and think sexy, sensual, and/or romantic thoughts, squeezing and releasing those PC muscles, while somebody (you or your primemate) skillfully touches your wet vulva, *and* if you don't get impatient with yourself—I can almost guarantee that you'll come. Gosh, I'm practically making myself come just writing about it. *Whew!*

Interestingly enough, the Latin root of the word "inspire" is *inspirare*, which means "to breathe." As you learn to breathe into your orgasmic state, you will not only have a much better time in bed, you will become an erotic inspiration to your primemate. Watch out, he may start calling you his "angel."

Give Him a Hand

Don't be afraid to ask for what you want sexually. Or just give him a *hand*—literally. Take your hand and push his hand, gently but firmly, to where you feel it will be most pleasurable. Or just touch yourself while he makes love to you. This might intimidate him at first (though most men love to watch a woman masturbate), but ultimately your freedom to do it sets him free, and *inspires* him. It also teaches him how to please you, so maybe he can do it a little better next time. The male loves to discover new sex "secrets." They inspire him to look for more.

Inspire Him with Your Imagination

Of course, don't confine inspiration to the bedroom. Amuse your man. Be his courtesan. Sing, dance, discuss his favorite topics, whether politics, sports, art, literature, films, spirituality, or his model train collection. Tell him stories. Remember Scheherazade, who saved her life and kept her king by spinning a different tale every one of 1001 nights. Now *that* was inspiration . . .

Light His Way

Inspire him with your goodness, your strength, your courage, your talents. Open up to him. Let him inside of not just your body, but your soul, your mind, your psyche. Be a beacon to him. Help him to evolve into a true gentleman who serves his lady, his muse, the light of his life. Give him the guidance that he needs. Give him words of inspiration, enlightenment, and encouragement, especially when he seems spiritually or emotionally lost.

Throughout the mysteries and mythologies of many cultures, the female is the provider of light. At the stroke of the Jewish Sabbath, the lady of the house is the one to usher in the holy day by lighting the sacred candles. In the Eleusinian mysteries of ancient Greece, the women carried torches, softly lighting the way toward growth and understanding.

Without the burning light of his lady, a gentleman's life is cold and dark indeed.

Recommended Reading

Castillejo, Irene Claremont de. *Knowing Woman*. New York: G. P. Putnam's Sons, 1973.

Moore, Thomas. *Soulmates*. New York: HarperCollins, 1994.

Sanford, John A. *The Invisible Partners*. New York: Paulist Press, 1980.

Stubbs, Kenneth Ray, ed. *Women of the Light: The New Sacred Prostitute*. Larkspur, CA: Secret Garden, 1994.

5

THOU SHALT

Excite Him

Keep him eroticized and just a bit off-balance. Complacency leads to displeasure. Remember: Gentlemen are natural hunters. One of their greatest pleasures, whether they know it or not, is the excitement of the chase. Make your gentleman constantly court you for your favors, and he will savor them all the more.

"Man is the one who desires," wrote Leopold von Sacher-Masoch[1] in his Victorian erotic classic *Venus in Furs;* "woman the one who is desired. This is woman's entire but decisive advantage." I don't see it as a lady's "entire" advantage, but it certainly is a vital one.

Drive Him to Desire You

Female pleasure is like a flower. It needs water (lubrication), support, warmth, sunshine. Male pleasure is like a car. It needs to be driven. Drive him to desire you. You excite him because you *are* his Holy Grail. You are what he is searching for. Understand your power.

---

[1] It is from Leopold von Sacher-Masoch that we get the term *masochism,* though your gentleman certainly needn't be a masochist for you to please him by exciting his desire for you.

> *In a great love affair, he is always on a quest for your love,*
> *even if you've been married fifty years.*

Always keep him aware that others want you. You don't have to actually go out with these "others," and, in most cases, you shouldn't (unless you're both into swinging or open relationships). Let him know you *choose* to be with him, but if you ever wanted to, you could have plenty of "action." You excite the male competitive imagination by being a "catch," desirable to others.

Benevolent Teasing

Tease him. A little teasing strengthens his love for you like a little exercise strengthens his muscles. Remember: The male needs to be teased because it makes him *slow down.* Exciting him often means slowing him down, sometimes even stopping him altogether, so his excitement can build and expand.

In the tender courtship stages of a relationship, a gentleman's excitement is ardent and delicate. If he's attracted to you, his desire for sex with you is almost instant. His arousal is urgent and compelling. It is easy to let his desire compel you and control you; but if you really want to excite him and keep him excited, you will take the wheel of his sexual convertible and *drive it at your own speed . . .* slow.

Sex Too Soon Can Shrink Excitement

If a gentleman engages in sexual intercourse too quickly in the course of a courtship, he (and you) may be thrilled for the moment, but that often sabotages the possibility of developing a deeper relationship. When the male reaches his sexual goal before he at least begins to fall in love, the hunter in him is so satisfied by his conquest that he may lose his drive to continue the pursuit. His climax may well be anticlimactic. Popular wisdom calls this having a "case of the windows": The gentleman looks at the lady sleeping next to him, then he looks out the window, and he wants to jump.

> *Delaying sexual intercourse allows the possibility of making love.*

Max and I knew each other for five years, then "made out" on the couch with our clothes on for six more months before we had sexual intercourse, and now we can't stop making love.

How to Turn a Gentleman on Without Taking Your Clothes Off

So, how to delay with panache? How to stay firm about postponing sexual intercourse while maintaining his excitement? How to turn a gentleman *on* without taking your clothes *off*? Don't "Just say no." That may have been a catchy phrase for drug control, but it's no way to put off sex when you're being courted by somebody you really like.

When a gentleman is turned down sexually, he generally assumes that either (1) the lady doesn't like him; or (2) she doesn't like sex.

Either way, he figures, there's not much future in calling and dating this woman, risking rejection, prudishness, hysteria, or all three. So, make sure you let him know you like him, and you'd like to see him again, giving him the message that he's got a chance in the future. Let him know you're attracted to him (if you really are), that you're a sensual woman, but that sexual intercourse is something very special for you, and you're just not ready for it *now*. Touch him—a little. Tell him you're enjoying getting to know him, and you'd like to get to know him better. Let him know that, although you might not be moving at the same sexual speed, you *are* moving in the same direction. Look deep into his eyes and, in your sultriest voice, quote the famous stripper Gypsy Rose Lee:

"Anything worth doing is worth doing slowly."

Try to come up with interesting, absorbing things to do on your dates, preferably in public places where it is generally easier to keep your clothes on. It sounds obvious, but the reality is that many people often wind up removing each other's clothing simply because they're home alone and can't think of anything else to do. Also, wear sexy, sensual outfits that are extremely difficult to remove. When I was dating, I used to staple my belts! Have fun, make out, but when in doubt, *kick him out!*

Keeping Things Exciting

So much for courtship. What about when you're already involved? If you love each other, familiarity will never breed contempt. But it can breed *boredom*, that "same old, same old" kind of feeling that can make even the most sincere gentleman, or lady, yearn to run off and get into trouble. So, no matter how well he knows you, there should always be a few mysteries you have yet to reveal, a few surprises up your sleeve, not to mention under your skirt. Think of Shakespeare's Cleopatra: "She makes hungry where most she satisfies."

Absence Makes the Heart Go Wander

Play hard to get occasionally, but don't be inaccessible. Many an otherwise hearty gentleman has been known to collapse from the exhaustion of the chase. The male needs to chase you, but if you completely disappear, he has nothing to chase. The reality is that absence doesn't make the heart grow fonder. *Absence makes the heart go wander.*

So, pay attention to him! Your kids, your career, your hobbies, your friends demand your attention, and they deserve it, but so does he. Keep in mind that very often, the male cheats not so much because he wants a new sex partner, but because his regular partner isn't paying attention to him.

Excite Him with Naughty Surprises

Wear surprisingly sexy lingerie. Call him at work and have phone sex. Role-play. Go out to dinner in an elegant dress and no panties. Write a hot letter and mail it to him at his office. Keep a diary of erotic fantasies and feelings and "accidentally" leave it where he can find it. Make him a video of yourself masturbating and entitle it "Thinking of You, Dear." Spark his erotic imagination. Actress Carole Lombard, the greatest love of Clark Gable's life, is said to have left a gift-wrapped, hand-knitted "cock-warmer" in Gable's dressing room with the note: "Don't let it get cold. Bring it home hot for me."[2]

Try taking sexual control of him. This can be direct or subtle, depending on the gentleman and on you. Your control might excite his fantasies, especially if he has a fetish for it. Or just experiment with new sexual positions, toys, outfits, ideas, attitudes. Remember, the

---

[2]Irving Wallace, *The Intimate Sex Lives of Famous People* (London: Arrow Books, 1981), p. 181.

first time you try something is not necessarily the best time. It's a learning experience. Just as the first time you ride a bike, you don't have your balance, the first time you try a new sexual activity or position, you haven't yet discovered the balance of your body parts. But don't do anything insane now, just for the sake of excitement!

> *Positive sexual development means knowing when you want to stop just as much as knowing when you want to go.*

Remember, you, and he, do have control over your sexual choices. The Devil doesn't *make* you do anything, darling.

Erotic Words, Dirty Talk

Hot talk excites most gentlemen. Cultivate a sexy voice, and use it to excite him.

So-called dirty words, because they're forbidden, carry a charge. They electrify our sexual synapses. If you find these words degrading and your primemate finds them exciting, talk to him about your feelings. Ask him about his. Is he really trying to degrade you? Or is it just that the words represent a certain wildness to him that's a turn-on?

Filmmaker John Waters, who had a strict, anti-sex Catholic upbringing, said, "Sex will always be better because it will always be dirty." If your primemate revels in the "dirtiness" of sex as Mr. Waters does, it's unlikely he'll change his attitude. Many gentlemen tend to get virtually locked into their sexual turn-ons. Often, they can't tell you why (though if you're persistent, you'll find out why). Basically, as far as they're concerned, *it's all about what gives them a hard-on.* Find out where his desires come from (a strict religious upbringing? being punished for childhood sexual explorations? early illness?), and you may feel less personally insulted by them and more free to play with them.

Flirt

A little tasteful public exhibitionism—dressing hot, dancing wild, or mild flirting—can be quite exciting to the visually oriented gentleman (unless you're saddled with a maniacally jealous or ultra-conservative male, in which case you'd better limit your excitement to your own bedroom). Just be sure that when you're flirting with others you keep it light and give extra special attention and reassurance to your primemate.

Let him know your show is for *him*. That's what I do with Max. I enjoy "flirting" with my audience through my radio and TV shows and Speakeasies, and Max loves to show me off by filming and broadcasting me. I also like to "play with" (dance with, caress, spank, or massage)[3] various female and male friends, all of which doesn't threaten Max since I reserve what we consider "intimate" sex (sexual intercourse, oral sex, French kissing, and other body-fluid exchanging activities) for him alone. And after an evening of that kind of light flirting and "outercourse," he and I often have a night of particularly exciting sex.

Different gentlemen have different thresholds of excitement tolerance. If you and your primemate can reach an understanding of what's "exciting," what's "threatening," what's "okay," and what's "definitely not okay," you will share a zesty, yet secure sex life.

Excite Him with Your Intelligence

Intellectual stimulation can be very erotic. It's not true that gentlemen don't like smart ladies—they do! They're just deathly afraid of ball-busters! So, don't bust his balls (unless he *really* deserves it); just tickle them. Your intelligence imbues your love life with humor, meaning, and excitement. His libido loves that, and his spirit needs it.

No Cheating

Share your excitement. If you have a monogamous relationship, don't cheat on him. That's right: *Just* don't *do it.* When you have a secret love affair, even if he doesn't know about it, he feels the loss of your excitement. Real infidelity is a betrayal, and that's not very exciting; it's depressing.

Certain gentlemen are very aroused by the idea of their ladies being with other men (perhaps because they find it a challenge to conquer their jealousy, or maybe the homoeroticism of the arrangement excites them), but only if it's in front of them, and then, *usu-*

---

[3]These are all forms of "extragenital stimulation," or "outercourse," very safe yet highly erotic forms of interpersonal play.

ally, only in fantasy. If you seriously wish to take this beyond fantasy, and your relationship is strong enough to handle it, you might want to try "swinging."

About Swinging

Swinging allows couples to explore the excitement of having sex with other people *right in front of each other*, which they feel is more open, honest, and better for their relationship than sneaking off and having affairs. For some, engaging in sex without commitment relieves pressure, makes sex a freer, wilder experience. Some people just really get turned on watching their spouse doing it with other people. Some enjoy the intimate camaraderie with other couples that the swinging or "playcouple"[4] lifestyle fosters. Actually, the reasons for swinging are as varied as swingers themselves. It's not for everybody. And swinging never made a bad relationship better. In fact, it usually makes it worse. But if your relationship is already very loving and trusting, and the two of you have high sex drives and a craving for adventure and novelty, it can be very exciting.

Novelty Is Exciting

The easiest way to have exciting sex is to do it with a new person. But you can add newness in other ways. You can do new things, add new toys, do "it" in completely different ways. In fact, you don't even have to *do* anything new. You can excite him by doing the same thing you've been doing for thirty years if you do it with passion, freshness, and your own genuine excitement.

> *Excite the male lust for variety with the multiple facets*
> *of your femaleness.*

Change your look occasionally. Vary your style from glamorous to sweet to intellectual to businesslike to spiritual to "slutty" (if you dare). Pretend that you are other women when you make love. Why would he want to be with other ladies when he has so many in you?

---

[4]The *playcouple* is the term coined by Dr. Bob McGinley of the Lifestyles Organization.

Of course, you're always really "just you," but let him see and feel the different sides of you.

What If He Can't Deal with You Being Too Overtly Exciting?

Most emotionally secure gentlemen love a lady who actively excites them. But some men are so obsessed with the traditional idea that the male must sexually dominate and initiate sex, and the female must passively acquiesce, that they feel intimidated and even humiliated when a lady is aggressively exciting. Then, again, perhaps *you* don't feel comfortable about directly initiating sex. Too bad. But don't worry, you can still be exciting. You just have to be a little mysterious about it.

Let your mystery ignite his mastery.

You can excite him by setting a sensual mood, wearing an erotic outfit, putting sexual items out—like a vibrator or massage oil—where he can see them. That way, you're not really initiating sex; you're just giving him exciting little hints that if *he* wants to initiate sex, you're ready.

If he doesn't get the hint, won't initiate sex, *and* recoils when you initiate, he may be exhibiting signs of what sex therapists call "male low sexual desire," e.g., chronic limp dick syndrome. Don't make a fuss about it at first, or you'll just make it worse. Just lie down next to him and play with yourself. That's exciting! If he's got a shred of desire left, he'll join in. If he doesn't join in, it's time to talk (not at that moment, perhaps). Often, the cure for male low sexual desire is as simple as adjusting his schedule. Then, again, it may require that he or the two of you talk to a sex therapist and/or a urologist.

Make Love, Not War

Do not try to excite him by participating in or condoning anything violent. Too many men in our society are raised to seek excitement and release stress in violence and nonconsensual domination.

Help him to seek his excitement and release his stress like a bonobo gentleman, in sensuality and pleasure, not in fighting and hurting.

If your guy is abusing you, you may not be able to simply stop him or get him to seek excitement and stress release in nonviolent activities. In such cases, your only solution, if you value your life, is to get out—the sooner, the safer.

Ripening Excitement Over Time

Sexual excitement and passion often burn out with age, but they don't have to. You can excite each other even when your tushy is sagging and his hair is thinning. Most long-term relationships go through up and down sexual cycles; that's normal. To keep the up cycles more frequent, *cultivate* the excitement just as you cultivate your garden. You know your begonias would die without nurturance; well, so will your sex life!

Recommended Reading

Owens, Tuppy. *The Planet Sex Handbook*. London: Tuppy Owens, 1995.

Nin, Anaïs. *Delta of Venus*. New York: Simon & Schuster Pocket Books, 1979.

Queen, Carol. *Exhibitionism for the Shy*. San Francisco: Down There Press, 1995.

Whipple, Beverly, and Gina Ogden. *Safe Encounters*. New York: McGraw-Hill, 1989.

Zilbergeld, Bernie. *Male Sexuality*. New York: Bantam Books, 1979.

The Lifestyles Organization Newsletter (Orange, CA).

6

THOU SHALT

Mother Him, but Not Smother Him

B̲e a source of nurturance and refuge to a man, and he'll love to be around you. Make him feel *at home* with you. All men need to be mothered. But men have experienced different mothers and so require different kinds of mothering.

What Is Pleasure-Mothering?

"Mothering a man" has such a negative connotation; most of the time it's used, it really means over-mothering, or smothering. But there is a loving, nurturing, *sexy* way to mother your primemate that I call "pleasure-mothering." What is pleasure-mothering? It depends on the man. For some men, all the pleasure-mothering you need do is let them suck on your nipples. For others, cooking for them, doing their laundry, spanking them, and reminding them to brush their teeth regularly isn't too much.

> *The secret of "pleasure-mothering" is to discover the level (almost constantly or just occasionally?) and kind (cuddling or coddling?) of mothering to which your particular gentleman is most receptive.*

Learn from the Great Mother—His

Learn whatever you can about how his real mother treated him. Guys want a gal just like the gal who married dear old Dad, and it wasn't just because she made a great meat loaf.

Don't get too excited, now. I'm not implying anything sleazy here. But Mommy did hug her little boy, kiss him, wash his tushy, and whisper sweet nothings into his ear. Or else she slapped him and screamed at him. Or maybe she ignored him. Or intruded upon his privacy. Whatever way she treated him, she was teaching him the meaning of love, doing a dress rehearsal for his relationship with you.

Probe him about his relationship with his mother, or lack thereof. Understand that often when he clashes with you (seemingly unreasonably), he is acting out unresolved conflicts with Mom. Find out what he loved about his mother and what he hated. Did their relationship feature more pleasure or pain? You don't have to be a psychologist to elicit this information and use it wisely to give him pleasure and maintain peace in your relationship. Talking about his mother is helpful not just to give you information, but also so he can see where he might project his deep, unresolved feelings about Mom onto you.

> *A gentleman's first impression of ladies comes from the First Lady of his life: Mother.*

Every man, no matter how strong, starts out as a helpless little baby, utterly dependent on "Mommy." She is all-powerful in his eyes, but she is by no means infallible. After all, even the most attentive mother is incapable of fulfilling all her baby's needs. The mother who provides love and nurturance also punishes and deprives. So the little baby boy begins to develop ambivalent, anxious feelings about her. She is sometimes the Good Mother and sometimes the Bad Mother, alternately the Good Witch of the North and the Wicked Witch of the West, the Goddess and the Bitch. Of course, at the same time that he is forming all these profoundly conflicted feelings about Mommy, he's forming comparably conflicted feelings about women in general.

Many gentlemen will deny vehemently that their mothers have had any influence on their attitude toward women. *Don't believe them*. Often, these are the men who have the strongest feelings about their mothers, and can't face the truth of Mom's tremendous power.

Mom and Sex

The sexual attitudes and behaviors of a gentleman's mother often have a strong influence upon his sexuality. If his mother caught him masturbating and punished him severely, he will probably have strong guilt feelings about sex. If Mom was a prude, he may feel that no "good" woman would enjoy sex. If Mom was flirtatious with him, he may develop strong fetishistic feelings about objects he subconsciously identifies with her, such as lingerie or high heels. If Mom was very intrusive into his private sex life, he may crave dominance from a lady. If Mom rarely touched him except to smack him, he may be drawn to sadomasochism. If Mom liked to hug, so will he.

Many gentlemen who enjoy sexual submission are reenacting scenes from their past with their original dominatrix, Mother—or a mother figure such as a nanny, teacher, aunt, neighbor lady—or fantasies of what they wish had been. If Mommy spanked her little boy, he may want you to spank him, too. If your gentleman prefers to be sexually dominant, it may reflect his continual desire to "top" the Great Mother.

Consider this: His very first sexual experience—being born—was with his Mom.

Know His Mom

If she's alive, get to know your primemate's actual mother, the lady that raised him. She can tell you a lot about her boy, if you dare to learn. In the folklore of almost all cultures throughout history, the mother-in-law is a figure of terror in the lives of wives. And well she should be, as she holds the key to her son's sensitivities. Even if you don't like her, you can learn a lot by studying her. You may learn something about yourself. You'll certainly learn a lot about how your primemate got to be who he is and why he needs what he needs.

Whether you like her or not, spend some time with her. Sit with her and go over his baby pictures. Get her recipes for whatever she used to cook that your guy liked as a little boy (I'm lucky: since Max's mom never cooked, I can make anything, and he likes it).

If your gentleman's mother is not alive or available, you're just going to have to get all your information about her from him (or maybe his other relatives). That means asking and listening. For a crash course in listening, see Lady's Commandment #5: Thou Shalt Listen to Her (page 39).

Why Gentlemen Need So Much Pleasure-Mothering

This commandment is by no means gender-exclusive; none of these commandments are. *We ALL need pleasure-mothering.* We all need someone special who understands how we feel and responds with tenderness. The typical feelings infants experience being held and fed—deep desires for physical and emotional bonding—stay with all of us all of our lives.

But many men, raised on society's notion that dependency needs, especially in males, are signs of weakness, don't want to admit they have these desires. Maybe that's why I put this commandment on the gentleman's side, because so many men in our society seem starved for mothering. In an effort to make them "strong," mothers tend to push little boys out of their laps earlier than girls, exhorting them not to cry or show vulnerability, forcing their "independence." This pressure often creates in the male a veneer of toughness with a core of even more profound neediness than most females have.

Even, perhaps especially, the toughest of men have baby needs. But often, out of shame of seeming "needy" or "feminine," a man won't directly ask to be comforted or taken care of. Rather, he may act out his need for mothering indirectly and even destructively, by getting sick, hurting himself or someone else, sulking, or throwing adult-style tantrums. If he's the type that won't tell you when he needs help, pay attention to his body language.

Learn to recognize signs of neediness in your primemate,
and give him a megadose of pleasure-mothering before he starts
acting out in a dangerous way.

Put him out of his misery! Sometimes, pleasure-mothering means having a quickie with him just to put him to sleep because it's late and he's hyper.

A Man, His Mom, and His Breast Fetish

Many an otherwise reasonable gentleman's life virtually revolves around his pursuit of the perfect breast (big or small, but usually big), the supreme bazoombah! Most "breast men" snort with denial if someone suggests that their interest in ladies' breasts might have something to do with their desire to be tiny infants suckling up to Mommy, but what do they know? After all, the glorification of the female breast as a *sex symbol,* as opposed to a maternal image, is so pervasive in our society. Probably the most "acceptable" contemporary American fetish is the one so many gentlemen have for ladies' breasts.

Though for some gentlemen, the adoration of the female bust seems to be *the* Holy Grail, it is, of course, a fetish, along the same lines as a foot or bun fetish, since the female breast is no more involved with actual procreation than the feet or buns. Breasts are far more essential to *nurturing* than to sex. And therein lies the infantile origin of the breast fetish. That deep need we all have for deep nurturance. Sustenance. Comfort. Food. The breast *is* food, after all. It is that unique part of a lady's body that actually creates food, the milk of life and love—and fetishes.

Most gentlemen enjoy lying against a lady's breast. Ladies like it, too; even heterosexual ladies like to lie on a man's chest, cozying up to its warmth and strength. But there's something about a female breast . . . We all, even if only in fantasy, long for a taste, a feel, a sniff of the female breast, so vital is it still to our sense of well-being. We yearn to be *nurtured,* whether we actually grew up with much nurturing or not. This yearning is so primitive, so obviously (and embarrassingly!) associated with infancy that many of us repress the longing out of a sense of shame that these are baby needs.

But the power of the breast is stronger than shame. Being held, suckled, babied, even the most uptight man may relax his control and let himself be lulled back to an infantile time that has a special, primitive pleasure. This is the original, ever-so-simple, mother/infant fulfillment.

> Can you remember how you felt as a baby
> snuggling up to your mother's big breasts?[1]

[1] All breasts are big when you're a baby.

I do. There's nothing like it. It's the ultimate comfort food. I also remember the feeling when she began to push me away. Horrors—the
ultimate, original rejection! All other rejections pale compared to
Mommy pushing my grasping, overage hands away from her vastly
overgrabbed breasts. It took me a long time to forgive her for that.
Some people never forgive their mothers. Some men never forgive
women in general for that first tragic rejection. They can only find
their peace when they lie against that breast that helps them feel like
a child again . . . sucking up to the maternal comfort that was once
denied them.

Your gentleman's need for pleasure-mothering may be very focused
upon your breasts. Teach him how to touch and suck them so that it
gives you as much pleasure as it gives him. Cuddle him at your breast
when he needs nurturance. If your breasts are large enough, you may
wish to try intermammary intercourse, or as the Latins call it, *coitus
a mammalia*, the act of ejaculating between breasts. The lady generally leans backwards as the gentleman places his penis between her
breasts and thrusts, the lady controlling the pressure by pushing her
breasts together. The vulgar term for this activity is "titty fucking,"
but I prefer the more elegant "pearl necklace."

A Notorious Breast Man

One of the most famous American breast fetishists was the notably
eccentric, hugely wealthy Howard Hughes. Hughes was an only
child and very attached to his doting mother, Allene, who died when
he was sixteen. He used his extensive power and money to seduce
hundreds of big-busted movie stars and showgirls in his passionate
search for the perfect bosom against which to rest his weary, neurosis-
ridden head. After viewing rushes of *Macao*, starring Jane Russell,
one of the buxom beauties in his "harem," Hughes wrote a three-
page memo detailing what kind of bra she should wear to enhance
her sumptuous bust.[2]

[2] Irving Wallace, *The Intimate Sex Lives of Famous People* (London: Arrow Books,
1981), p. 227.

The Power of Pleasure-Mothering

Pleasure-mothering can be almost as powerful as real mothering. It can be fantastic therapy, better than sitting in some psychiatrist's office and talking about your mother complex for an expensive hour or so a week. If your primemate was hurt or shamed as a little boy by an overly intrusive, abusive, or negligent mother, or even a "good" mother who just made mistakes like we all do, you can now do a lot to heal his old wounds through pleasure-mothering.

Different gentlemen do crave different kinds of pleasure-mothering. But almost all men need to be hugged and cuddled, just as women do, though some poor guys are uncomfortable with touching that isn't directly sexual or aggressive—at first.

> *You can teach a man to appreciate touch, if you have the patience and feel that he's worth it.*

Hold your primemate in your arms, rub his shoulders, stroke his head like a child and tell him how much you love him, or whisper into his ear how you're going to do kinky, raunchy things to his body, combining pleasure-mothering with excitement and fantasy. Soothe him when he's in pain, let him cry when he needs to, comfort him when he experiences a loss, and when he succeeds, celebrate with him like a proud, supportive mommy. A good pleasure-mom is like a great coach, cheerleader, nurse, and sexy sex therapist rolled into one.

And don't worry: Pleasure-mothering like this won't turn him into the proverbial "big baby," quite the contrary. Providing for the occasional dependency needs of the little boy in him actually helps him to be more of a healthy, happy, grown-up gentleman.

But Don't Smother Him

When mothering is overdone or out of line for a particular man, it becomes smothering, making him feel overwhelmed, overfed, nagged to death, swallowed up, consumed, even castrated. Men love to be taken care of. But they want to be strong. They can't bear being completely helpless (except, perhaps, for an occasional bondage game). So don't be all over your primemate all the time. Be a bit mysterious.

> *It is every man's pleasure to be free.*
> *Let him be . . .*

Balancing independence with closeness, freedom with restraint, dependency with autonomy is an important pleasure point, and one of the keys to a happy, healthy, long-term love affair.

When Might You Be Smothering?
So, at what point does mothering become smothering for your primemate? When does nurturing become nagging? Your gentleman will have times when he needs to talk, other times when he needs to be left alone. He has times when he craves a cuddle, other times when he needs to jog around the block or be with his dog. Study his patterns, what seems to make him feel better, and under what circumstances. Ironically enough, sometimes you can draw a gentleman out of his shell by simply leaving him alone. After a while, he will miss you and come back to you, if you let him know you'll welcome him when he does.

> *Experiment with your mothering behaviors as you might with*
> *recipes—see what he likes, see what makes him sick to his stomach.*

Take note of which mothering gestures irritate or insult him. Often they remind him of something that really irked him about his own dear mama. Does he hate when you remind him to do things, otherwise known as *nagging?* When you fuss over his eating, drinking, or smoking habits? When you criticize his fashion choices? When you cuddle up to him while he's trying to concentrate on something? When you tell him not to do dangerous things? When you ask too many questions about something he doesn't want to talk about? When you try to take over his life (for his own good, of course)?

If it's a behavior you can give up easily, like worrying about whether his socks match, give it up. If it's very important to you, like wanting to communicate about serious issues or needing more cuddles in your life or stopping him from gambling away your mutual savings, then you need to discuss it with him. Of course, you may just want to forget about this guy altogether. Please don't waste your life trying to rescue someone who is determined to destroy himself and anyone close by. But if you think he's the "perfect gentleman" for you in every other way, you can try coming to terms with him. Talk about your needs, ask about his. Listen, and try to understand him.

Pleasure-mothering is almost as central to a good relationship as making love. If your pleasure-mothering style doesn't mix well with his needs, and vice versa, you'll either split up before long or make each other miserable. If they do mix well, then you and he will know the pure ecstasy of pleasure-mothering.

Recommended Reading

Goleman, Daniel. *Emotional Intelligence*. New York: Bantam Books, 1995.

Scarf, Maggie. *Intimate Partners*. New York: Random House, 1987.

Solomon, Marion. *Lean on Me*. New York: Simon & Schuster, 1994.

7

THOU SHALT

Discover His Deepest Desires

and Fantasies

Gentlemen love to explore their sexual fantasies. If your man doesn't do it with you, he'll do it with somebody else (or at least, he'll want to). Find ways you can weave his fantasies, along with your fantasies, into your sex life, even if that just means talking about them.

You may find pleasing his deepest desires as simple as wearing a garter belt and stockings, or maybe just letting him wear the garter belt and stockings (depending on the man).

Don't be a sexual saint, though; don't do anything that really turns you off or causes you pain. Let him know your sexual limits, e.g., "Vaseline is okay—gasoline is not okay." But do try to be open to things that don't hurt you.

If you explore fantasies together, you've pressed a precious pleasure point in his body and soul that he won't easily give up.

Where Does Fantasy End and Reality Begin?

Fantasy makes up a major part of human consciousness. The English philosopher John Richter pointed out that "Fantasy rules over two-thirds of the universe, the past and the future, while reality is confined to the present."[1] Memory, as it filters through the mind's eye, is a kind of fantasy that looks toward the past. Hope and anticipation, fear and ambition are fantasies that look toward the future. Our sexuality is fueled by fantasies of the past *and* the future.

Where Do Our Fantasies Come From?

Your erotic fantasies begin in the cradle, sometimes even in the womb. By the time you reach your teens, they get really intense. Your fantasies usually come from the first sexual images you find arousing—your mother's lingerie, your father spanking you, catching your sister naked in the bathroom, your brother wrestling you to the ground. That's why you might have incest fantasies. But don't worry; just having incest fantasies doesn't mean you're an incest perpetrator or victim. Most people have incest fantasies and never act on them.

You might also pick up sexual images from school experiences, as well as from your favorite fairy tales, movies, TV shows, popular music, not to mention sneaking a peek at Daddy's *Playboy* and checking out the lingerie ads in *The New York Times*. These images are very powerful, because they impress themselves upon you when you're very young and impressionable. They become blueprints for your sexuality, repeating themselves in your memories and activating your imagination. They infuse your natural sexuality with meaning and excitement. And they become fantasies.

Our fantasies are the G spots of our minds.

What Are Fantasies Good For?

Sexual fantasies are good for lots of things. They can be relatively harmless mind-rehearsals for sexual acts you haven't yet experienced. They can be safe outlets for dark, forbidden desires that you can't or wouldn't want to live out. Sexual fantasies can release a little of the steam from that big balloon of adulterous desire so you can maintain your monogamous relationship without blowing up. One alternative to the manifold complexities of nonmonogamy is maintaining an active fantasy life with as many partners as you can imagine.

[1]Quoted in *The New Dictionary of Thoughts*, compiled by Tryon Edwards (New York: Standard Book Company, 1955), p. 192.

For Max and me, fantasies are great mental sex toys, interactive mind-movies. While making love, we sometimes become partners in imagination for a joint venture in sexual adventure, using fantasy scenarios to heighten the romance of our monogamous reality. We have favorites, of course, and we always get new ideas from my callers and sex therapy clients. Which reminds me:

So many of you have thanked me for enhancing your sex life. . . .
Well, Max and I would like to take this opportunity to thank you
for enhancing ours!

Actually, with fantasy, you can have two kinds of sex at once. In reality, you may be having "regular" sex, while you whisper a much wilder fantasy, maybe an orgy scene, into each other's ears. The fantasy of being in an orgy might be very exciting, though in reality, you'd be horrified if your primemate had sex with other people! Sharing fantasies allows you to experience every imaginable, erotic delight without risking your health, safety, or monogamous relationship. It's one of those things that helps keep love alive as long as your imagination lasts.

Sharing fantasies can be pure, unanalyzed fun, but it can also be serious psychic exploration, similar to working with dreams. You can use your fantasies to learn about yourselves and the deep sources of your erotic natures. You can "work" with your fantasies, role playing and discussing them, to help the two of you grow and change.

When Not to Share

Some fantasies shouldn't even be talked about, if telling them would hurt your primemate, or cause him to want to hurt you. For instance, if you have fantasies of having sex with an old boyfriend and your guy is the jealous type, these are *not* fantasies to share. You certainly do not have to tell everything. The more you can tell, however, the more you can play with, and the closer you'll be.

How to Fantasize Together

If you've never shared a fantasy with your lover, and you'd like to try, start by sharing a memory, an exciting sexual experience you actually had together. Reminisce about it in bed, then embellish the memory by imagining something that could have made the experience even more exciting.

> *Be poetic, be explicit, be romantic, be outrageous, be honest,*
> *be whatever turns the two of you on.*

You can also stimulate sharing fantasies by reading erotica together, listening to erotic audiotapes, or watching an erotic video. Watch *The Dr. Susan Block Show* together—that'll stimulate your fantasies!

Do not tell your primemate, "We need to spice things up." He will instantly feel inadequate. Just start talking about something sexy, a story you heard or read, a memory or one of your fantasies that you think he'd enjoy, as you stroke or kiss him. Then get him to embellish, or ask him what he likes to think about when he makes love or masturbates. Or just show him this commandment, and say, "Well . . . ?"

If he opens up and tells you a special, private fantasy that shocks you or you don't quite understand, don't mock him or get angry with him. If you don't think you're capable of handling whatever he comes up with, better not to ask. If, however, he tells you something that excites you, let yourself go. . . .

Erotic Role Playing

Sometimes you have to become "strangers" to get closer. Sometimes playing roles that aren't "really" you brings you closer to yourselves.

Erotic role playing lets you be whoever you want or whatever he wants you to be. You can be a hooker, a virgin, a princess, a superwoman, a goddess, a slut, a nurse, a man, a little girl, a tiger, a space alien, a bonobo chimpanzee—*anything*. Dress the part, if you like, and use props. Create a sexual psychodrama. You may want to film some of your sexual role plays, creating your own personalized video-erotica (great to watch on other, less creative occasions).

Or just talk and feel your way through a fantasy. You can spin a powerful spell with nothing but the sound of your sultry voice. Whisper erotic images into each other's ears while you make love. You can also share them through phone sex when you're apart. Actually, the physical limitations of the phone encourage you to verbalize feelings and fantasies that you might be shy about revealing in person. You can also write fantasy notes and put them in his briefcase for him to discover. Leave them on his answering machine. Or communicate fantasies by E-mail.

Sexual fantasy provides a chance for adults to play. Children use fantasy all the time when they play. You can use fantasy role play, too, right in the erotic "sandbox" of your bedroom. If you want to turn sharing fantasies into a game, both of you can use slips of paper to write down the fantasies you're curious about but afraid to bring up. Put the papers in a hat. Pull one out and talk about it. If you feel brave, role-play it, or as musicians say, "riff on it." If not, just talk about it. Or pick another. Try past-life regression fantasy play. Go into a light trance, taking you back into a "past life." Describe what you wear, who you are, where you live—Renaissance England? Ancient Egypt? Roaring Twenties? Cold War Fifties? Free Love Sixties? Weave a sexual fantasy into that character and time period. Play music to fit the mood. Talk with an accent. Go wild. Have fun.

All Great Fantasies Don't Translate into Great Realities
Be careful about acting out certain fantasies in real life, especially if they involve other people.

Many things are better in fantasy than in reality. It might be fun to imagine making love in the jungle, but the reality of doing that would involve mosquito bites and malaria.

> In fantasy, everything's perfect. Reality has a way of breeding insects, diseases, jealous husbands, and hysterical wives.

Yet if you really want to act out your fantasy, enjoy! Far be it from me to stand in the way of your orgiastic adventure. Just practice safe sex, keep your wits about you, and try not to hurt anybody, including yourself.

How Embarrassing!
What if it doesn't hurt, but just embarrasses you? That's an odd area, because embarrassment can be truly mortifying, a real passion-killer, or it could add to the excitement. It could also be something you need to "work through" in order to develop your erotic nature. Talk to your primemate about your feelings. Or just feel the embarrassment, and do it anyway! At least, try it once. Confessing your embarrassment sometimes diminishes it or, under ideal circumstances,

can even transmute embarrassment into a turn-on. Of course, if your embarrassment or discomfort is truly profound, don't traumatize yourself. Just relax, take a deep breath, tell your primemate how you're feeling, and try another, less threatening path to sexual fulfillment.

Almost Every Gentleman Has Fantasies . . .[2]

The Perfect Woman

From early adolescence on, almost every gentleman has fantasies about sex with a passionate, beautiful, exciting lady who will do what he wants, even if that means dominating him. She may be a gorgeous model type, a raunchy slut, an innocent young virgin, an experienced older woman, an androgynous seductress, a girl-next-door, or a powerful dominatrix. She changes as he does.

> *She is, quite simply, whatever he wants her to be, and she does whatever he wants her to do.*

As such, she is "perfect." However, she's no direct threat to you, because she doesn't exist—except, in a sense, as the erotic anima of his imagination. But ignore her at your peril! Get to "know" her if you want to pleasure your man. Explore her. Role-play her. Challenge her. Expose her. Whatever you do, "deal with" her in some way because if you don't, he will search (like the proverbial knight on his hunt for the Holy Grail) for someone who will.

Two Ladies

> *Double your pleasure, double your fun,*
> *Sex with two ladies is better than one!*

Well, at least, it's one of the most common male fantasies. If you have bisexual fantasies, you can have a ball playing with this one, pretending that the two of you are making it with another lady or

---

[2]For more erotic fantasies, see Lady's Commandment #10: Thou Shalt Find Out What Her Dreams Are Made Of (pages 71–84).

two or three or a whole cheerleading squad—hey, why stop when you're just fantasizing?

Whether to take it from fantasy to reality and actually invite another lady into your bed is a big question. Usually, the answer is to keep it in the realm of fantasy. But if you and your primemate are both great sexual adventurers, trust each other implicitly, know how to play safe, and have talked it out sufficiently so that you *both* feel comfortable and ready (neither of you should be pushing the other), you may want to go ahead and try this classic male fantasy.

Domination

Most gentlemen dream of having their way with the ladies, that is, dominating them. Power is a great aphrodisiac! Many men in our society are brought up on sports and competition, and so they associate pleasure, even erotic pleasure, with winning and dominating an "opponent." This may be a distortion of love and sharing, but *fantasy usually involves distortion*. Many men like to "win" at sex, to master, to be on top, to score, to drive home their phallic point with hard-pumping power. This is a traditional male fantasy that influences most popular pornography.

Males who always like to dominate sexually are often underachievers in the real world. They are releasing their frustration at the lack of control they have over their lives by exerting a high, very theatrical kind of control over their sex partners. If you like to take on the submissive role and your primemate likes to dominate, you're ready to play.

Gary, one of my sex therapy clients, has domination fantasies that he often plays out with his wife, Leah. He fits a dominant male "profile," being a very bright male with a master's degree who works as a car salesman. Until Gary was fourteen, his father beat him regularly, giving him hard, bare-bottom paddlings that made him cry with pain and humiliation. Gary also watched his older sister receive the same abusive treatment, and he was torn by feelings of horror for her pain, excitement over her burgeoning sexuality, and relief that *she* was the one being punished, not him.

Such an upbringing could easily move a man toward violence and abuse of his own children or wife. But Gary has managed to create a peaceful life for himself. As a teenager, he got into a few fights, but as an adult husband and father, he has learned self-control. He channels his (now minimal) violent impulses into playing safe but exciting domination scenes with Leah, who enjoys the thrill of submission. Together, they act out dark memories and fantasies. Sometimes Leah dresses up like a schoolgirl, and Gary puts her over his knee and spanks her before they make love. Or she puts on slave garb, and he ties her up and whacks her bottom with soft leather whips that don't really hurt but make loud, cracking sounds. Sometimes he "makes" her "worship his cock."

Gary still has many unresolved conflicts about his abusive upbringing, but he is determined never to be violent with anyone, certainly not his own three young children. Role playing his domination fantasies with Leah helps him to express his feelings in a controlled way. Since Leah was also brought up with spankings and even went to a school that practiced corporal punishment, she too is working through her own sadomasochistic fantasies as she role-plays with Gary.

If your primemate has dominant fantasies, play them out only within your comfort zone. Once again, don't do anything that really hurts you. Don't let anyone "dominate" you that you don't feel certain has all his marbles, as well as your best interests at heart. Being sexually dominant is one thing; being domineering and abusive is another. The red flag that should warn you not to surrender, not to trust, but rather to get the hell out of the situation, is any kind of physical or verbal abuse, unless you really want to be a miserable victim, which some people do, but I don't want to encourage it. The key feeling you get with an abusive partner is *fear*. Not fantasy fear—*real fear*. Basically, bad people, like bad governments, get their way through fear and intimidation. Good people, even if they're dominant, don't have to really frighten their partners to get them to surrender; they negotiate for power with love.

Submission
The other side of dominance is submission. Many gentlemen fantasize about being a sex object—being seduced, spanked, ravished, even raped, or "forced" to perform various sexual acts. It may sound silly to some women, considering how many ladies balk at being con-

sidered sex objects, but lots of men crave it, within certain boundaries, of course.

Many women are frightened by their male primemate's submissive fantasies. They are afraid that because he craves surrender, he is not much of a man. They think he must be some kind of wimp or weirdo for wanting that. In reality, many powerful men do yearn to submit sexually. Many of my sex therapy patients who have submissive fantasies are successful businessmen, weary of their responsibilities and stresses. They long to be infantilized, objectified, to be taken advantage of, to surrender control for a brief period in their day or their week, a vacation from responsibility and a time trip back into a childhood under someone else's, usually a woman's, control.

Many submissives just want someone sexy to push them into doing things they're afraid to do on their own. Some find that a little fantasy fear increases sexual arousal. Many submissive men long to surrender to an exciting woman who knows what she wants and isn't afraid to demand it from them. Some like anal penetration, the body's ultimate surrender. Some respond to fantasy humiliation, being called names or "forced" to do embarrassing things. Some like to be spanked, sometimes, though not always, because they were spanked as children.

His fantasy may be that you're an Amazon leather queen and he's your sex slave. Or you're a schoolteacher, he's a student, and you teach him a lesson in love. Or you're a nurse, and you erotically examine him. Or perhaps you're a mother figure who does naughty, nasty things to her little boy. Or maybe you're just a bitch and he's a sucker. For more on why *you* might enjoy dominating *him*, see Lady's Commandment #10: Thou Shalt Find Out What Her Dreams Are Made Of (pages 79–81).

Of Male Bondage

Why does a gentleman enjoy being tied up? One (usually subconscious) reason is that it allows him to relax and not feel guilty about enjoying sex. After all, what can he do? He's all tied up! Some men find it removes performance anxiety. If you can't move, you can't perform, so what's to be anxious about? Some men love to struggle against restraints, building a rush of adrenaline. Gentlemen who are much stronger than their partners, but still want a passionate exchange of physical power, like being restrained so they can feel that thrill of being overcome and overwhelmed sexually.

WARNING: Bondage, like mountain climbing, skydiving, and driving a car, can be dangerous if not done properly. Take your time with it. If neither you nor your primemate has done it before, start simply. Don't tie anything too tight. Make sure things like circulation are in working order. Don't tie anything around the neck, and don't leave anyone in bondage by themselves for more than a few minutes.

Exhibitionism and Voyeurism

Many gentlemen enjoy the thrills of watching, and some enjoy being watched, too. Please don't equate exhibitionism with public exposure. When I use the term, I just mean showing off sexually for people who *want* to watch.

The stereotype is: ladies show off, men watch. But ladies can enjoy erotic entertainment, and gentlemen can have a great time stripping for ladies. If you think your male primemate might have a secret exhibitionist fantasy but is too shy to speak up about it, take the initiative. Buy him some sexy underwear and say, "Honey, put these on. . . . Ooo—that's sexy. . . . Now take them off . . . slowly . . ."

Sebastian, one of my therapy clients, has had a recurring fantasy for the past few years. He's in the center of a group of about a dozen lovely, lingerie-clad ladies, all lying around on pillows sipping wine, eating oysters, playing with vibrators and dildos, and kissing and licking each other. They're also watching him dance for them. He's completely naked except for one leather collar around his neck and another around his hard-on. The ladies command him to shake his hips, bend over, bark like a dog, and masturbate for them, until they all come at once, vibrators buzzing, and sperm shooting everywhere.

When he first came to me, he couldn't imagine doing anything about this fantasy except to obsess over it in the privacy of his own psyche. After all, he was, and still is, a highly respected network television executive and more conservative about his lifestyle than a minister. (This meant I couldn't propose moonlighting as a Strip-O-Gram dancer as a solution to his frustration.) So I suggested that he try sharing his fantasy with his wife of eleven years, with whom he had a "decent but dull" sex life and "great" communication.

This took some coaching. First, we determined that the most important element of the fantasy was not the number of ladies but the fact that they were watching him dance, masturbate, and generally make a sexual spectacle of himself. So we downsized from a dozen to one: his wife. I suggested he prepare the scene for her (pillows, wine, oysters, sex toys for her to play with), get himself a couple of leather collars, and go to it. At first, he thought I "didn't know his wife," but he was intrigued enough to discuss it with me for several weeks. He and I went through every step in the fantasy scene, doing little verbal dress rehearsals, to give him the courage to actually go through with this. He kept saying that his wife wouldn't get into it; she'd think he was certifiably weird; she'd probably just take the kids and leave him standing with nothing but two leather collars around his big and little heads. . . .

After about a year of trying to forget his fantasy and realizing he couldn't, as well as considering hiring twelve hookers and resolving he wouldn't, he decided to risk domestic excommunication and share it with the wife, just as I suggested. Can you guess how she reacted? Not only did she "get into it," but she went farther than he'd dreamed, attaching a leash to both of his leather collars and leading him around the bedroom! Now their whole sex life has blossomed, but no, they haven't invited over eleven other ladies. Actually, they don't even "do" the fantasy that often. They just whisper it into each other's ears as they have sex, which isn't so "dull" any more!

> *What fantasy could your male primemate be harboring deep*
> *in his psyche that he's afraid you won't like?*

Maybe you should ask. You might like it, and it might give a much-needed boost to your sex life.

Bisexuality

What if your male primemate is fantasizing about having sex with other males? This is common. It's a big secret, especially among heterosexuals, but it's true:

> *Many men think about men, especially their cocks.*
> *Especially big cocks.*

Remember, ladies don't have penis envy, gentlemen do. Even—perhaps especially—outwardly homophobic men have gay fantasies.

This doesn't necessarily mean they're "really gay." Masters and Johnson reported that heterosexuals often fantasize about homosexual encounters, and vice versa.[3] Their studies and others have shown that this reflected curiosity more often than the desire to change the gender of one's real-life lovers. Norman Mailer went so far as to say that "There is probably no sensitive heterosexual alive who is not preoccupied with his latent homosexuality."[4] I would add the phrase "at some point in his life," since such fantasies are not necessarily ongoing.

Male same-sex fantasies also often reflect a desire to do something forbidden. Randy, one of my clients, was having a tough time with Beth, his fiancée, whom he said he loved but was scared to marry. In the months leading up to the wedding, he found himself fantasizing about having hot, taboo sex with abnormally well-hung men, without commitments, without questions, without love. He didn't want relationships with men; he wanted a relationship with Beth. But he couldn't stop thinking about guys with big cocks. What he really needed to do was share this secret fantasy with someone because that would make it a bit less taboo, taking some of the edge off. After he shared it with me, I coached him into sharing it with Beth. Now she wields a mean strap-on dildo, and they're both happy campers.

If your primemate has homosexual fantasies, it may also represent a desire to make love to himself, to explore and celebrate his maleness. In a way, he is attempting to "bond" with his own masculinity. Sometimes male same-sex fantasies express a longing to connect with a father who may have been distant. Then again, if he constantly fantasizes about being with other men, it *could* mean that he is more homosexual than heterosexual, and his relationship with you is part of his effort to deny his true feelings.

Your partner may express his homoerotic desires through fantasizing about you having sex with other gentlemen. He may imagine sharing you with lots of guys—a consensual gang-bang! This can be great for you if you like fantasizing about being with other men.

[3]William Masters and Virginia Johnson, *Human Sexual Response* (Boston: Little, Brown, 1966).
[4]Norman Mailer, "The Homosexual Villain" in *Advertisements for Myself* (New York: G. P. Putnam's Sons, 1959).

Careful about taking this fantasy into reality, though. Usually, it's best left in the Theater of the Mind.

Same-sex fantasies can be threatening to a heterosexual lover. Keep in mind that, though our society tends to make things black or white, good or bad, male or female, liberal or conservative, heterosexual or homosexual, the human sexual imagination is most definitely *bisexual*.

Fetishes

Fetishes combine body parts (feet, breasts, hair, etc.) or objects (shoes, leather, panties, etc.) with desire. Often, all kinds of fantasies are projected onto the fetish object. People with fetishes can have "normal" sex lives: just incorporate the fetish into sex. If your prime-mate has a foot fetish, you're a lucky lady. Get him into acupressure massage and you'll have toegasms galore!

Cross-Dressing

Ladies, if you should find a pair of lacy panties and silk stockings stashed in a hidden compartment of your husband's briefcase, don't jump to conclusions. They may not be another woman's, but his!

Cross-dressing is nothing new. From ancient Greek drama to Victorian Bloomer Girls to modern drag queens, ever since men and women started wearing different clothes, they found excuses to wear each other's clothes. Currently, unlike men, women who wear "male" clothing have few social problems. Tomboys are accepted. Sissies are not. It doesn't seem fair, but such are the decrees of sexual fashion.

How does male cross-dressing start? Every cross-dresser has a different story, but most begin their lifelong love affair with feminine apparel around early adolescence. The first glimmers of the fetish often revolve around Mama's sensual, forbidden panties. Many teenage boys get aroused by touching or smelling Mom's or a sister's lingerie, usually hanging tantalizingly over a towel rack or lying nestled in a hamper. Cross-dressers take this common interest a step further, as they actually put the stuff on.

Why do they do it? They feel it's exciting, relaxing (even tranquilizing), mystical, dangerous, irreverent, erotic, and more. Some simply want to be ladies. Some are gay, but *most are straight*. Many say they feel that deep inside, they are lesbians. One of my clients, a firefighter who has trouble connecting with women, dresses up so he can *be* the kind of lady he'd like to go out with, but can't find. Then there's James, a retired judge (born male), who just married Sharon, an attorney (born female). It was a beautiful wedding: James wore a full-length bridal gown, and Sharon wore a top hat and tuxedo.

Why are so many closet cross-dressers judges, firefighters, construction workers, police officers, attorneys, and CEOs?

Usually, they are overcompensating for or trying to "disguise" their desire to be feminine by going into a field that is traditionally ultra-masculine. Many feel that ladies are pampered. Whether that's accurate is irrelevant. The fact is when these men cross-dress, *they* feel pampered. They forget the stresses of the office, fire station, construction site, or whatever "masculine" thing they do, and relax. It's funny—psychologically, I know why dressing like a woman helps a "tough" guy relax, but physically . . . well, when *I* want to relax, I take *off* my high heels and garter belt, and put on a T-shirt and shorts!

Most experts say the desire to cross-dress starts as a sort of security blanket when a boy seeks comfort in Mother's clothing to escape a harsh or absent Dad. If he's caught in the act, he's often humiliated, which makes him feel guilty, but enhances the excitement of cross-dressing. Some say cross-dressing is partly genetic.[5] Regardless of the cause, most experts agree that the desire to cross-dress is not something someone can simply eliminate, even with therapy, especially if it's been going on since childhood.

The biggest problems arise when cross-dressers feel they must stay in the closet, which most do. Many of my cross-dressing clients have girlfriends, or even wives of twenty years, they wouldn't dream of telling about their undercover fashion passion. I understand their desire to keep it secret, since the potential for stinging rejection or worse is immense in our society. But I know cross-dressers are happier and healthier—and less likely to get into trouble—if they can share their fetish with someone they're close to.

[5] Simon LeVay, *The Sexual Brain* (Cambridge, MA: MIT Press, 1994), p. 131.

If your male primemate is cross-dressing, try to keep an open mind. Listen to what he has to say. You may want to go together to a sex therapist who specializes in this area. Though cross-dressing itself is tough to change, with a little knowledge and a lot of love, wives have been known to modify the way they deal with their husband's fetish. Usually this requires modification on the husband's part as well, not necessarily of the cross-dressing itself, but of some other aspect of his behavior toward his wife. Keep in mind that though many women are horrified to discover their male primemate's cross-dressing, some not only tolerate it, they love it. You may, despite your assumptions, find that you enjoy it, too! And hey, if your sizes aren't too different, you can trade panties.

Go Ahead, Be Naughty

A lot of boys are brought up to think of sex as dirty, nasty, forbidden. Therefore, their psyche "needs" sex to be "dirty" for it to be hot. Often, such men think they can't really enjoy sex with their wives because marital sex is too proper in their minds, unless the wife has a "dirty" imagination.

One of my therapy clients, a midwestern churchgoing dentist, likes to imagine he's driving his Mercedes around the worst part of town when he picks up a hooker—and not just any hooker but a nasty, filthy-mouthed streetwalker with ripped stockings and wild eyes. They pull over to a back alley filled with trash and winos, and they have sex right on the sidewalk, crescendoing with the hooker pulling his wallet filled with money and credit cards right out of his pocket, and running away. This fantasy—from pick-*up* to rip-*off*—is a major turn-*on* for this man, to the point where when he first spoke to me, he was thinking about going to Vegas to see if he could make his fantasy a reality.

I advised him to stay home and just enjoy the fantasy. Whew! Sometimes, making your dreams come true is wonderful, but in this case—NOT. I'm trying to get him to talk to his wife about it, so they can role-play the whole dirty, nasty, fearful thing in the safety of their bedroom. But, as of this writing, he's afraid to tell her.

What fantasy is your male primemate afraid to tell you?

Fantasy Evolution

Your primemate's fantasies will evolve and change as he does. If you and he can "air" and explore them in a safe manner, they will tend to lose their obsessive quality. As you share your evolving fantasies, you will weave powerful strands into the fabric of your relationship, blending fantasies with memories and ever-expanding possibilities.

Recommended Reading

Anonymous. *My Secret Life*. Atlanta: PND Books, 1967.

Anonymous. *The Pearl*. New York: Ballantine Books, 1973.

Bannon, Race. *Learning the Ropes: A Basic Guide to Safe and Fun S/M Love-making*. Los Angeles: Daedalus Publishing, 1992.

Cleland, John. *Fanny Hill: Memoirs of a Woman of Pleasure*. New York: Carroll & Graf, 1990.

Friday, Nancy. *Men in Love*. New York: Dell, 1980.

Garber, Marjorie. *Vice Versa: Bisexuality and the Eroticism of Everyday Life*. New York: Simon & Schuster, 1995.

Love, Brenda. *The Encyclopedia of Unusual Sex Practices*. Fort Lee, NJ: Barricade Books, 1992.

Luther, Jeanette (Mistress Antoinette). *Tied Up with Love*. Orange, CA: Versatile Publications, 1988.

Miller, John, and Kirsten Miller, eds. *Lust: Lascivious Love Stories and Passionate Poems*. San Francisco: Chronicle Books, 1994.

Steinberg, David, ed. *The Erotic Impulse*. New York: G. P. Putnam's Sons, 1992.

8

THOU SHALT

Remember What Thy Mama Said:

"All Men Are Little Boys"

Every man has at least a bit of Peter Pan in him. It may be obvious, as in what the Jungian analyst Marie-Luise von Franz calls the Eternal Boy.[1] Or it may be deep inside a man, locked away in a mental closet—or maybe a subconscious steel-plated vault! But it's always there.

Some men are so competent and powerful as professionals, husbands, and fathers, you'd hardly know there's a child inside. But no matter how old he acts, he was young once, and his youth is still within him yearning to break free in some way.

Draw out the little boy in him. Play with that little boy, talk to him, and he will delight you with his innocence and enthusiasm.

Understanding the Little Boy Helps You Deal with the Sexual Man

Find the little boy inside your man. Take him by the hand, figuratively and perhaps literally. Talk to him about his childhood, help

[1]Marie-Luise von Franz, *Puer Aeternus: A Psychological Study of the Adult Struggle with the Paradise of Childhood* (Santa Monica, CA: Sigo Press, 1970).

him to deal with the good and the bad. Talk to him about his fantasies, the games he plays in the playpens of his mind. Our sexual nature begins to form when we're infants. Understanding the little boy inside him will help you to deal with the sexual man.

Good Boy/Bad Boy

Whether the child inside is a good little boy or a naughty, nasty little boy depends on the man and his mood. You'd better be able to handle that little boy one way or another.

Some of the most mature, responsible, dependable gentlemen get tremendous pleasure out of being naughty, mischievous little boys in some way. In the words of Victorian bad boy Walter Bagehot:

> *"The greatest pleasure in life is doing
> what people say you cannot do."*

There's nothing quite like doing and thoroughly enjoying what other, lesser mortals say is impossible, improbable, immoral, or inappropriate. Help your primemate to channel his desire to be "bad" into something creative or, at least, relatively harmless like whitewater rafting, rollerblading, composing a nasty rap or speed metal song, or having a quickie in the middle of a workday.

"Boys Will Be Boys"

"Men are little boys" does *not* mean "boys will be boys." There's no excuse for bad behavior. There is a big difference between being child*like* and child*ish*. Don't let him get away with violence, irresponsibility, rudeness, or selfishness. Support the expression of his juvenile masculinity only in ways that do not hurt anybody.

Play with Him

Boys love to play. Your guy might like physical play or verbal play. While some men prefer to play alone, most need playmates. If you really want to give a gentleman pleasure, play with him, learn to play his favorite sports and other games. Become his primemate-playmate, the best buddy of that little boy inside of him. Of course, he may need you to be his mommy, too, sometimes. All boys need mommies—*sometimes*.

Babytalk: The Language of Love

Use babytalk, or at least "pet names," with your primemate. All stressed-out adults yearn to be babies again, at least occasionally. The easy, artless "art" of babytalk lets you feel that way with your partner, giving you both a mini-vacation from the pressures of adulthood, allowing you to cultivate the frolicsome joys of innocence well into old age. If your primemate finds it difficult to speak "as a man" about his deep vulnerabilities, e.g., tell you he loves you, tell you he's hurt, tell you he's sorry, tell you he needs your help—he may be able to say it in his own personal dialect of babytalk.

Boys Like Toys

Boys tend to look at everything as toys, or "objects," including their lovers, at least occasionally. Try not to resent this aspect of men; play with it. There is power for you in mastering (or mistressing) this game. As long as you don't do anything that hurts you, it's okay to play the role of boy toy/sex object every once in a while, to play out his fantasies, especially if you can make them dovetail with your own. Even feminists like me do it. But watch out, you may find yourself enjoying it!

Phallic Toys

"Sometimes a cigar is just a cigar," said Freud, but sometimes it *is* a phallic symbol. Boys adore phallic toys. Our civilization is filled with them, large and small, from ballpoint pens to the World Trade Center. Bombs, rockets, and guns (the real and toy variety), undeniably of more interest to boys and men than to girls and women, bear an unmistakable resemblance to an erect ejaculating penis—any boy's favorite toy.

Gun control might best be served by encouraging men to deal with their boyish needs for phallic play without violence. Help your male primemate to enjoy *non*violent phallic toys—pens, paintbrushes, hammers and nails, screwdrivers (now there's a great name for a phallic tool!), telescopes, telephoto lenses, golf clubs, sports cars, motorcycles, airplanes, dildos, vibrators—not to mention his own fabulously phallic dick!

Sex Toys

Many gentlemen enjoy sex toys. Does yours?

Your primemate's interest in sex toys may be bringing you closer together or pushing you apart. Many couples playfully use adult films and other erotica, as well as vibrators, dildos, flavored lubricants, French ticklers, leather whips, lingerie, feathers, satin sheets, velvet pillows, handcuffs, and cameras, to enhance their sexual pleasure. They might call phone sex lines together or go to strip clubs together, using these services as "sex toys" or sexual enhancements.

Then again, your guy may be using sex toys and even people (e.g., hookers, strippers, women he doesn't care about) as a distancer from sexual intimacy with you. In this case, the toy is used to escape closeness, not to enhance it.

Every boy needs a little escape once in a while, but if your primemate would *usually* rather watch a porn movie and diddle himself with his butt plug than have sex with you, you probably have a relationship problem. You may have to haul him out of virtual reality and get him back to real reality; that is, pull his *plug* and talk.

When you talk, be careful that you don't act like his mother and reprimand him for watching "filth." He will resent the hell out of you, pull further away from you, and sneak his little sex toy sessions when you're not around. Instead, remind him that you are his playmate, and he can have a much better time *sharing* his fun and games with you.

Try to be fair with him. If he's playing with toys, sexual or otherwise, to avoid being with you, consider how your behaviors and attitudes may have contributed to "driving him to it."

> *Have you been rejecting his sexual advances? Have you been denigrating his sexual interests? Have you been ignoring his fantasies and desires?*

Sex Toy Obsession

If your guy has been playing with sex toys—human, high-tech, cybernetic, latex, or celluloid—*obsessively* since before you got to know him, he may be stuck in a serious sexual rut. This kind of behavior is difficult to overcome, though not uncommon among men. Our masculinist society pressures little boys to disassociate from their mothers and everything feminine at a very young age in order to be "masculine."

Little boys learn early on that the worst, most humiliating name they can be called is "girl" or "sissy."

They go through a period, generally from about age eight to thirteen, when they look down on girls. At this age, callousness, even sadism toward anything soft and female is considered cool. Intimacy is scorned. Love is disdained.

Most boys grow out of this phase, at least to the extent that they can get involved in a serious, intimate relationship with a lady. Most boys learn to love again. But some boys don't. They may grow up and date women, they may get married, they may even "fall in love" after a fashion, but they never stop scorning everything feminine. These men often focus their sex drive on sex toys—porno films, prostitutes, blow-up dolls—anything they feel they don't have to respect, but can still "get off" on. According to Freud, such men have "Madonna-Prostitute" complexes, seeing "good" women as asexual and sexual women as "bad." Even if they do manage to fall in love with a lady, these men find it extremely difficult, if not impossible, to combine their feelings of love with sexual excitement. With serious sex therapy appropriate to their situation, men like this *can* change and learn to love, respect, and be aroused by the same woman. But usually they don't change, because, for the most part, they have no desire to change. Don't get involved with a guy like this if you value the quality of your sex life.

Quickie Power

Most little boy-men, even the sensitive, loving ones, like fast, fun, easy (for them), light, impersonal sex, at least every once in a while. Long-lasting, intimate, foreplay-rich sex is just too much "work" for them to do every time they get horny. So, if he's a "good boy" and deserves it, give your primemate an occasional "quickie." Quickies are great for satisfying male horniness, reducing stress, getting him focused, and for putting your "little boy" to sleep in the middle of a restless night.

Bonobo Sex Tactics

Consider how our cousins, the bonobo chimpanzees, use sex to reduce tension or violent conflict. When one bonobo gets upset with another bonobo, the second bonobo may just give the first one a nice blow-job to calm him down. Well, you can do that, too. You too can use pleasure to create peace.

Now, I sincerely hope that your male primemate never uses violence with you or anyone else. But if he gets upset and cranky in that unreasonable, whiny, little boyish way, why not just put him out of his (and your) misery, make like a bonobo chimp, and suck him off? I know it sounds pretty crass, but hey, it works for the bonobos, and it works for me and Max, not to mention hundreds of couples that I've counseled in living the Bonobo Way, and it might just work for you and your precious "little boy." Of course, sometimes he won't "let" you do this; he wants you to take his tantrum seriously! But sometimes, it hits the spot like a cold beer on a hot day.

Recommended Reading

Farrell, Warren. *Why Men Are the Way They Are*. San Francisco: Berkeley Books, 1988.

Gray, John. *Mars and Venus in the Bedroom*. New York: HarperCollins, 1995.

Kiley, Dan. *The Peter Pan Syndrome*. New York: Avon Books, 1984.

Miedzian, Myriam. *Boys Will Be Boys*. New York: Doubleday, 1991.

9

THOU SHALT

Regard Him as a Hero

Every gentleman yearns to be a hero, even if just to one person in his life: you. It sounds corny, but it's absolutely true. "All men are possible heroes," wrote the nineteenth-century English poet Elizabeth Barrett Browning.[1] Every man wants to be Superman with all those superpowers (except, of course, the part about being faster than a speeding bullet!).

Give your male primemate your admiration, and he will give you his devotion. Let him help, protect, and defend you in whatever way he can, and don't forget to express your appreciation—loud and clear now!—when he does. Modesty notwithstanding, *pride* is one of every man's greatest pleasures in life. He may or may not like the word "hero," but he'll like the way he feels when you let him know you're proud of him, because you touch a very sensitive pleasure point: the male ego.

His Life Has Meaning

Whether he's a captain of industry, a courtroom warrior, a champion of the Right or the Left, a really good neighbor, a minister to those in

[1] In *Aurora Leigh* (1857), Book 5.

need, a marathon man, a wonderful dad, or a great artist—whether he does heart transplants or generator transplants—make him feel that his life has meaning, import, and worth, not just to you, but to the world. If it didn't, or at least didn't have heroic potential, you wouldn't be with him, right?

A Modern Male Identity Crisis

Of course, ladies need to be regarded as heroines, but the contemporary male's heroic needs are particularly acute. Many modern gentlemen are terribly confused about their roles in relationships. They *used* to be *the* providers and protectors in the family. But now, many ladies can provide for themselves, make their own money, and fight their own battles. Modern women can be their own heroes, and many men feel left out. Some really feel knocked for a loop. Some get pretty loopy, lashing out against the ladies in their lives. Some become violent. Others become gentlemen.

This doesn't mean that ladies should stop being heroines, or providing for and protecting themselves and their families; not at all. It just means that you have to make an extra effort to let your male primemate know you need him, that whatever he provides is greatly appreciated. Whatever he does to protect and defend you (short of gratuitous violence) is heroic.

Value His Help
Don't take anything he does for you for granted. If you don't show your appreciation for the things he does for you, he'll soon get sick of doing them, and probably he'll get sick of you, too. When you let him know you appreciate and truly value what he does for you— even the little things—he'll be motivated to do much more.

Be Sensitive to His "Heroic" Hang-Ups
Support him at vulnerable and embarrassing moments. Most gentlemen, raised to think they always have to be "tough" and "in control," are far more sensitive about being embarrassed in public than most ladies. Pass up opportunities to make him look bad or to exacerbate an already humiliating situation for him, and deep inside he'll know you're *his* hero.

Also be sensitive to his "heroic" rescuing complex. When you have a problem and you complain about it to your male primemate, you may think you're just letting off steam, but *he* thinks he has to rescue you. Many gentlemen have this complex. They like to solve the problem, bring home the bacon, and rescue the maiden. When you just need to talk about a problem, let him know, loud and clear, that it's not his fault, and that he doesn't have to rescue you.

Make Him Feel Heroic in Bed

You may not be able to tell him he's the "first," and there's really nothing heroic about that, but you can tell him he's the best. He's not? Well, I wouldn't want you to lie, but he must be best at something. If not, give him a copy of these commandments and make him the best.

The modern gentleman must work much harder in bed than men of the past. He must prove he's not a selfish macho asshole *or* a limp wimp by engaging in personalized creative foreplay, and maintaining his erection without coming too quickly or too slowly. The least you can do when he gets it all "right" is to show and tell him how great he is.

Treat him like a hero, praise him, pump him up.[2] It's good for him, like vitamins.

Support Him in Nonviolent Heroics

Do not define his heroism in terms of violence, except in self-defense or the defense of you and your family.

Honoring all other kinds of violent "heroism" begets more violence.

He doesn't need that, and neither does our society.

Let your primemate know that he is heroic because of his strong values, good heart, and courageous spirit, not because he picks fights. His heroic qualities include his initiative, independence, determination, character, curiosity, creativity, and courage. They do *not* include insensitivity, brutality, eagerness to fight and get into trouble, a hardened attitude toward sex, or an obsessive need to dominate and win.

---

[2]In Italian, the word *pompino* (slang translation: a blow-job) literally means "to pump him up."

The medieval troubadour ideal of a "gentle manhood" celebrated those virtues of tenderness and bravery that touched the hearts of the ladies. Gentlemen are not wimps.

> *One can be a sensitive and caring hero.*
> *And one can be a wimp and control an army.*

Ladies can make a big difference in male violence. If women don't encourage, reward, and glorify violence, far fewer men will engage in it. Ladies always have power over gentlemen, the power of sex. In Aristophanes' fifth-century B.C. play *Lysistrata*, the ladies of two warring provinces, Athens and Sparta, withhold sex from their husbands until they stop their endless, senseless war. The men are outraged, but in the end, holding throbbing hard-ons in their hands instead of spears, they finally consent to stop killing each other. Sex and peace are everyone's reward.

Help him, by encouragement and example, to be an *ethical* hedonist, a true bonobo gentleman, one who savors, cultivates, and *gives* lots of pleasure, and tries not to hurt anyone, including himself.

Recommended Reading

Johnson, Robert A. *He: Understanding Masculine Psychology.* New York: Harper & Row, 1977.

Wright, Robert. *The Moral Animal.* New York: Pantheon Books, 1994.

10

Thou Shalt

Swallow

. . . at least sometimes. For most gentlemen, swallowing is a symbolic acceptance of "all of him," as well as an essential aspect of oral sex, a physical joy, and a spiritual symbol. A communion of sorts. For the male, semen is a holy, precious fluid. It is the creamy "milk" in our erotic Land of Milk and Honey.

The combination of orgasm, ejaculation, and feeling his precious primemate swallowing his precious semen is an ineffable male pleasure.

Swallowing is an act of surrender. A gentleman surrenders *as* he comes; you surrender *to* his come.

Swallowing can also be an act of power. Cleopatra was said to be a great swallower. Rumor had it that she fellated dozens of her soldiers in one night. That's one way to make sure the military is on your side. . . . Yet many ladies have a very hard time with this (pun intended), which can pose a bit of a sexual problem. After all, *some* gentlemen might dislike being sucked to orgasm, but I've never met either one of them.

If you're finding it difficult to accept your gentleman's come in your mouth, it could be for any number of reasons, some solvable, some not so solvable. Following are a few possibilities:

Swallowing Hang-Ups and How to Handle Them

1. You Think It's "Dirty"

If you mean "dirty" in a literal way, you should know that a gentleman's penis, being so rarely exposed, tends to be one of the cleanest parts of his body. It's certainly cleaner than his mouth, and you don't mind kissing, do you? If your primemate is healthy, his semen is healthy. Semen—produced by the testicles, the seminal vesicles, and the prostate—consists of a tasty combination of protein, citric acid, fructose, sodium, and chloride, with just a touch of ammonia, ascorbic acid, calcium, cholesterol, and other minerals and chemicals. See, no dirt. In fact, the ammonia could clean your sink! According to the Kinsey Institute, the total volume of semen in each ejaculate is around one teaspoon and contains 120 million to 600 million sperm. The average ejaculate has only five to fifteen calories, so even dieters don't have to worry.

But back to "dirty." If you mean "dirty" in a spiritual sense, perhaps you've had a religious, sex-negative, genital-shaming upbringing. Without meaning to offend your religion, let me just say that *I* believe that going all the oral way with someone you love is an exciting act of intimacy, and yes, an act of corporal communion, with nothing unclean or obscene about it. Messy maybe, but not unclean.

2. You Find It "Degrading"

Hmm. Maybe you're reading too much Catharine MacKinnon or Andrea Dworkin. Maybe at some point in your life, you were *forced* to go down on someone. That's terrible, of course, and you should allow yourself to heal. But don't take too long; life is too short to spend it as a victim. And don't deprive your current guy because of what past guys did to you. Though if your *current* guy is forcing you to do anything, honey, he doesn't deserve for you to follow any of these commandments, and you should get the hell out *now*.

3. You're Afraid of Catching a Sexually Transmitted Disease

Actually, this is a pretty good reason *not* to swallow. With the possibility of contracting HIV and any number of other sexually transmitted diseases from semen, many experts consider swallowing a gentleman's come to be a high-risk activity.

If you're at all uncertain of your gentleman's physical health, put a

condom on him. For oral sex, use the nonspermicidal kind; that spermicide tastes nasty! There are some fairly good-tasting mint and
chocolate-flavored condoms you can try. You can even put one on
with your mouth. Take the tip of the condom in your mouth, unroll
it with your fingers, stretch it a little, put the tip of the penis to your
lips, and release the condom over the cock. You can also let him
ejaculate *on* some other part of your or his body, your clothes, or into
a towel (Max and I call it the "terry-cloth condom").

Save come-in-your-mouth communion for a gentleman you love
and are sure of. As long as your primemate is truly healthy and not a
carrier of HIV or other diseases, you need not be afraid of swallowing.

4. You're Afraid of Gagging to Death

I've never heard of a woman who has indeed gagged to death on a
mouthful of semen. But I've talked to lots who fear it. Please let me
reassure you: As long as he's not one of those macho jerks who
pushes your head like he's dribbling a basketball, *you* are in control
when you give head, not him. Play with him at your own pace. However, though his semen won't gag you, his penis might. Just remember that you don't have to deep-throat the thing continuously to
make him come in your mouth. *If* he starts ramming it down your
gullet despite your protestations, just bite it—hard, if you have to—
and he'll stop.

The most sensitive part of a gentleman's penis tends to be the head
and the rim around the head, so you can spend lots of gag-free time
holding the shaft in one hand or two, depending on your gentleman's
size, and happily sucking and twirling your tongue around that head.
Use lots of your own slippery saliva to ease the sucking. If you have a
dry mouth, drink some water before you suck. Ice water will give him
an ice pop cock! As adult film star and fellatio expert Nina Hartley
says, one secret to good cocksucking is a "happy mouth." If your
mouth is happy, your man will be.

5. You Don't Like the Taste

You can improve the taste of a man's semen by making sure he eats
or drinks certain things, like cinnamon, pineapple juice, or celery
(see Lady's Commandment #2: Thou Shalt Stimulate Her Senses, for
recipes, page 17). No asparagus, though; asparagus has a way of making all your body secretions taste rancid. Meat tends to make semen

taste salty. Rice and grain ferment in the stomach and can make semen taste a bit rank. Milk and protein shakes may make it thicker in consistency. If you're up for a little taste testing, experiment with how different foods and spices affect the flavor and texture of his ejaculate.

If you just can't stand the taste of his semen no matter what he eats, or if you don't want to change what he eats because you're trying to "accept him for who he is" *and* for what he eats, take some advice from Mary Poppins: When you feel like he's fairly close to coming, apply a little honey, chocolate sauce, or other gooey, yummy stuff to his throbbing member, then suck and swallow away.

If that's too messy for you, you can develop your oral skills so his ejaculate shoots directly down your throat, bypassing your tongue and taste buds, and you'll hardly taste a thing. Just think of it as the oral sex equivalent of shotgunning a beer!

You could even put a little extra salt on the rim.

6. *Your Lips Get Tired*

If your gentleman takes a long time to come, whatever the cause, this could be a very legitimate reason for you to prefer not to keep on suckin' until he does. In fact, you could find yourself with a painful case of fellatio lockjaw if you overdo this. Fortunately, I have a fairly simple solution: Mix oral sex with *aural* sex. That is, you suck on him a while, then talk to him a while—tell him a sexy story, tell him you love him, talk dirty, or whatever you and he like—while stroking his penis manually, then go back to sucking and so on. Mixing aural and oral sex means your lips won't get tired, though you may wind up talking with your mouth full!

7. *You're Just Too Tired in General*

Get some rest! Or just do it when you're up for it, say, in the morning. Most gentlemen tend to come faster in the morning anyway, so morning blow-jobs require less stamina on your part. Let him service *you* at night. If you follow even some of these commandments, you deserve it!

Recommended Reading
Jong, Erica. *Fear of Flying*. New York: Harper & Row, 1973.

Dr. Susan Block's
10 Commandments *of a*
Gentleman's Pleasure
(Abbreviated Version)

I Thou Shalt Accept Him for Who He Is . . .
. . . not for what you wish he could be. You can change little things, but not big stuff. If you simply can't accept him, you probably shouldn't be with him. And you certainly shouldn't bother to follow all these commandments for him.

2 Thou Shalt Adore His Penis
Gentlemen love their own penises, and so should you. His penis is not just his greatest source of pleasure, it's his identity. Explore his other erogenous zones—his buns, nipples, feet, lips, ears—but you can't focus too much affectionate attention on his precious penis. Love it in sickness and in health, in hardness and in limpness. Basically, the more harmoniously the three of you can live together, the happier all of you will be.

3 Thou Shalt Be a Source of Beauty in His Life
You don't have to be model-perfect. Just find out which parts of your body he likes, and accentuate their beauty. Dress for sex, at least occasionally. Love your body. Be a pleasure to his eyes, and he'll never take them off you.

4 Thou Shalt Inspire Him
Be a beacon of light in his life. Your intelligence, beauty, and integrity are inspirations to your gentleman. But your pleasure is his great-

est, and your *sexual* pleasure is his *sweetest* inspiration. *Men work to get laid,* either by someone special, the whole world, or something in between. Inspire him to work, to live, to love, to please you.

5 THOU SHALT EXCITE HIM

Men are natural hunters and love the excitement of the chase. Keep him eroticized and just a bit off-balance. Complacency leads to displeasure. Keep him aware that others want you. Excite him with naughty surprises.

6 THOU SHALT MOTHER HIM, BUT NOT SMOTHER HIM

All gentlemen need to be mothered, but men have experienced different mothers and so enjoy different kinds of mothering. The secret of "pleasure-mothering" is to discover the precise level and kind of mothering to which your particular gentleman is most receptive.

7 THOU SHALT DISCOVER HIS DEEPEST DESIRES AND FANTASIES

Men love to explore their sexual fantasies and fetishes. If your gentleman doesn't do it with you, he'll do it with somebody else (or at least he'll want to). If you can discover and enjoy erotic fantasies together, role playing or just talking about them, you'll press a precious pleasure point in his body, mind, and soul that he won't easily give up.

8 THOU SHALT REMEMBER WHAT THY MAMA SAID: "ALL MEN ARE LITTLE BOYS"

With some gentlemen, it's obvious. With others, it's very deep inside, locked away in a mental closet. But it's always there. Draw out the little boy in him, play with him, talk to him. And remember: All boys like toys. Boys tend to regard everything as toys or "objects," at least sometimes. Don't resent this aspect of your gentleman; play with it.

9 THOU SHALT REGARD HIM AS A HERO

Give him your admiration and he will give you his devotion. He may not like the word "hero," but he'll like the way he feels when you let him know you're proud of him, because you touch a sensitive pleasure point: the male ego. Never define his heroism in terms of violence, except in self-defense or the defense of you and your family.

10 THOU SHALT SWALLOW

. . . at least occasionally. For most men, swallowing is a physical joy and a spiritual symbol. A communion of sorts. If *he's* clean, his come is clean. If you're not sure he's clean, skip this one. Save come-in-your-mouth communion for a gentleman you love and are sure of.

Epilogue

God concluded His Ten Commandments with "the thunderings, and the lightnings, and the noise of the trumpet, and the mountain smoking. . . ."[1] I'd like to conclude mine by giving you a thundering and lightning lifetime orgasm, a smoking stroke of multiple pleasures that makes you trumpet your joys to the world! As the pioneering orgasm advocate and psychotherapist Wilhelm Reich said, "The pleasure of living and the pleasure of the orgasm are identical."[2] I exhort you to:

Go forth, and give pleasure!

Give an orgasm, an eargasm, or a deep, sweet soulgasm to your primemate tonight. Use the commandments in this book to guide you down the path of his or her many special pleasure points. Use them to find the bridges between your differences, then walk, run, drive, or dance across those bridges into paradise.

Are you ready for paradise?

Do all those pleasure points and all these commandments seem

[1]Exodus 20:18.
[2]Wilhelm Reich, *The Function of the Orgasm* (1927), Chapter 5.

like a lot to follow? Are you *ready* for all this giving? Are you ready to share your life with another human?

Is your beloved primemate worthy or capable of receiving all this love and pleasure? Perhaps you're not even with anyone you would call a "beloved primemate" at the moment. For one reason or another, most people will not or cannot follow all these commandments all the time. That's the reality of life.

If you can't follow them all, don't worry. I won't strike you with lightning or send you to hell (my organization isn't that powerful). But the more of these commandments that you can and do follow, the closer you'll be to your Land of Milk and Honey. If you follow just a few, well, at least you'll get a trickle of milk and honey.

Practice the Bonobo Way of peace through pleasure wherever you can in your life, but especially with your primemate.

Be wild, be free, but please, be ladies and gentlemen. Practice ethical hedonism. Pursue, cultivate, and share the myriad pleasures of life, mental and physical, and try never to hurt anyone, including yourself. Remember:

The power to give pleasure is the greatest power you have.

Acknowledgments

It is my great pleasure to thank:

My marvelous partner-in-love, a pioneer in the fields of erotica and human sexuality, my beloved husband, Prince Maximillian Rudolph Leblovic di Lobkowicz di Filangieri (that's only about half of his names, but I don't want to get ridiculous here).

My first teacher in the art of loving: my wonderful, beautiful, creative, supportive mom.

My very special brother, Steve, who test-drove the hottest passages of this book by reading them on the intercom at work.

My super-suportive superagent, Peter Miller of PMA, along with the always helpful Yuri Skujins and Harrison McGuigan.

My fine, unflappable editor at St. Martin's Press, Heather Jackson, for her enthusiastic belief in this book, from the beginning.

My loyal lawyer and dear friend, John Levine, for his useful input and support.

Dave Longtin, Dana Solta, Sharon Scrot Shore, John Guttierez, Lawrence Friedlander, Adele Framer, and Willem de Ridder for proofreading help and editorial feedback.

The "Bonobo Gang" of The Dr. Susan Block Institute for the Erotic Arts and Sciences: Bobbo Martinez, Nigel and Adrian Morier, Michael Leblovic, Elyssa Weinstein, Efrem Logreira, Ben Schlaver,

Kiki Moretti, Stephen Whetstone, Paige Hart, Roxanne Milner, Snake Eve, and Slave Louanne, for helping keep the show and the Institute together as I wrote this book.

Asha Mallick, Ken, Virginia, Angela, Maya, and the always charming staff at the Century Wilshire Hotel, a delightful environment in which to write and make love.

National Public Radio, Keith James and KMAX, and all the other courageous, discerning radio folks who have put *The Dr. Susan Block Show* on the American airwaves.

Sheila Nevins, Dave Bell Sr., Dave Bell Jr., Shari Cookson, John Moss, and all the other exceptional ladies and gentlemen working with me from HBO and DBA on the new TV show.

The great teachers of my life, especially Marjorie Merklin of Harriton High, Robert Brustein and Bart Toiv of Yale University, Allen Ginsberg and Chogyam Trungpa Rinpoche of Naropa Institute, Stan and Ann Rice of San Francisco State, and Simeon Wade of Pacific Western, who taught me to analyze, dramatize, lyricize, and appreciate life and its infinite pleasures.

The spiritual guides of my youth, Rabbi Ivan Caine and Rabbi Gerald Wolpe, for helping me to think conscientiously about the original Ten Commandments and all the divine complexities within that great international best-seller, the Bible.

A few more very special ethical hedonists I'd like to thank for their general, all-purpose support above and beyond the call of friendship: Joe Ravetz, Al Goldstein, Mark Anthony and Susan Thomas of *Dream Dresser*, Dr. Michael Perry, Cat Sunlove, Carol Queen, Joani Blank, Mark Greenblum, James Wohl, Lena Syphers, John Clark, Diane Block and the extended Block clan, as well as all my mom's fabulous, loving friends.

And to my radio and TV audiences—as well as all my splendid show guests, students, clients, and *Dr. Suzy's Speakeasy*–regulars—a more elaborate "thank you" is in the *Prescription for Pleasure* that opens this book. But I just want to let you know again: I love you more than I can say. . . .